# RARE BREEDS

# RARE
# BREEDS

Photographs by Robert Dowling
Text by Lawrence Alderson
Introduction by Roger A. Caras

A Bulfinch Press Book
Little, Brown and Company
Boston · New York · Toronto · London

Frontispiece: **Dark Dorking cockerel**

First North American Edition

Designed by Mikhail Anikst
This book was produced by Calmann & King Ltd, London

ISBN 0-8212-2125-6
Library of Congress Catalog Card Number 94-75735

Bulfinch Press is an imprint and trademark of
Little, Brown and Company (Inc.)
Published simultaneously in Canada by
Little, Brown and Company (Canada) Limited

PRINTED IN SINGAPORE

# Contents

### White Park

This head exhibits all the appeal and distinctiveness of White Park cattle. The strong black markings of the muzzle, ears and eyelashes set off the pure white background of the face, and are enhanced by the classically shaped horns which grow sideways before curving gracefully forwards and upwards. The head of a White Park bull was chosen as the symbol for the Rare Breeds Survival Trust in Great Britain because the breed combines the elements of historical significance and sentiment with those of commercial characteristics and genetic uniqueness, thus epitomizing the philosophies of the Trust.

# Acknowledgements

It would have been impossible to create this book without the help and advice,
given most generously, of a large number of people.
The photographer, author and editor would like to extend their thanks especially to
Pat Cassidy, Editor of The ARK,
the staff of the Rare Breeds Survival Trust at Stoneleigh,
the staff of Rare Breeds International,
David Bradley and the Temple Newsam Estate,
Bernard and Shirley Hartshorn and Wimpole Home Farm,
Hollanden Farm Park, Cotswold Farm Park, Toddington Manor Farms Limited,
the British Pig Association, Mr and Mrs Oakley of Rede Hill Farm,
Laurent Avon of the Institut de l'Élevage,
Annick Audiot of the Institut National de la Recherche Agronomique,
Dr Jurgen Gunterschulze of the Tierpark Warder,
Dr Antonio Rodero of the University of Cordoba,
Donald E. Bixby of the American Livestock Breed Conservancy,
Caroline Hadley of the Domestic Fowl Trust,
and Bob Ault and M. and S. Shimwell of the National Federation
of Poultry Clubs' Championship Show.
We would also like to thank the many breed secretaries and individual breeders
who gave so freely of their time and expertise in helping us
to organize the photography of the animals. They are too numerous to list here,
but their assistance was invaluable. Details of those
whose animals are featured in the book are given on pages 141–3.

# Introduction

by Roger A. Caras

Here, at the end of the twentieth century, our species has stopped, taken a deep breath and begun to wonder. What have we done? In heaven's name what are we doing? Dare we continue?

The inventory is terrifying. Some of our planet's richest topsoil has been degraded, eroded, and is vanishing. The Earth's forests have been wasted in a most profligate way. Even our atmosphere is rotting, no longer able to protect us against cosmic radiation. Surface water (and heaven alone knows how much sub-surface water), has been poisoned. Acid rain is turning sweet water and sweet soil sour.

Nowhere, though, is this dreadful litany more appalling to the senses than when it is applied to other species of animals. We have already learned to live without a vast number of plants that should really have been cherished and explored, but biodiversity, the animal part of it, the engine that drives evolution, is shrinking, becoming less diverse by the hour and that does frighten us. This, at least, is true of those of us with enough brains to think about such subjects as survival and eternity.

When we think of other animals in trouble on this planet, we have been conditioned to think of wildlife, tigers and salamanders, elephants, rhinoceroses, aye-ayes and butterflies. The mountain gorilla, the lemurs of Madagascar and the chimpanzee, creatures disturbingly close to us in kind, are all the more disturbing because they may be gone very soon indeed, and that does more than give us pause. It is appropriate that we should be very concerned. The world's wildlife is a precious heritage which we have been squandering, and we must bring things back under control. It is strange, though, that all of our concern seems to be extended solely to those animals that live apart from us (wise choice, we must concede), and so often little thought is given to those immediately at hand, the species we ourselves guided into being once their wild ancestors had yielded up to domestication.

In fact, uncounted breeds, varieties and geographical races of domestic animals are also vanishing at a bewildering rate. Even though we can reach out and touch them, literally, even though they dwell in our paddocks, live in our barns and eat our fodder, we have done so little in the past and are doing far too little now to arrest this plunge into oblivion by the very creatures that gave us our present high station in life.

Of course there are groups striving to head off disaster (and extinction is disaster, or at least a disastrous misuse of priceless gifts). Globally, there is Rare Breeds International,which coordinates the activities of national organizations such as the Rare Breeds Survival Trust in Britain, and the American Livestock Breeds Conservancy and Joywind Farm Rare Breeds Conservancy in North America and Canada, all fighting a worldwide trend, and in doing so they make it impossible for us to plead ignorance. It is happening, we know it is happening, and we will never be able to deny it. These organizations have put us on notice, as have the rare breeds themselves.

Just what is a domestic species? There are approximately 35 of them, ranging from silkworms and honeybees to the familiars of the farmyard: pigs, poultry, horses, cattle, sheep and goats. Their domestication made it possible for us to rise above the hunting and gathering stage of our development and achieve some of the first breakthroughs in human technology. Without them there would have been little or no meaningful technology beyond the skills of violence, hunting and warfare.

In our pre-agriculture stage, the Mesolithic or Middle Stone Age, we domesticated our first four animals while we still were using caves! The goat probably came first, and the sheep could have been second. (It could, in fact, have been the other way round the osteological evidence is inconclusive, since it is impossible to distinguish at least the long bones of goats from their counterparts in sheep. Without other evidence, such as a skull or horns, we can't be sure.)

That's two, the others? The dog, no big surprise there, and reindeer! All that before we were out of the cave. And what a difference that one idea, domestication, made to our future. With beasts of burden there could be caravans, trade, urban centres, universities, technology. The way was open.

Take just that first species, the goat. In the world today there are between 60 and 65 distinct breeds, as well as scores of often very limited geographical varieties. Between three and four billion goats – the poor man's cow – are now held by people on six of the seven continents. The Anglo-Nubian and the British Alpine (the United Kingdom's version of French, Italian, Spanish and Swiss Alpines), the British Saanen and the Toggenburg are familiar enough in the British Isles, as are their counterparts in North America, but what of the scores of others?

A breed or even a type of domestic animal is an artifact. It represents not only the genetics of ancestral forms but tells us far more about the human animal than most of us realize. There is the matter of taste. Not everything we have built into our favoured domestic breeds is utilitarian, far from it. When we look at a horse, carefully devolved from wild forms for over six thousand years (the goat may go as far back as twelve to fifteen thousand years), we are looking not only at a form that can carry a rider or pull a cart, we are looking at a form that pleases. A horse is the history of aesthetics. We pictured them on cave walls, in petroglyphs and on bits of antler and bone, then we took them into our lives and let them transform us. Domestic breeds are history itself. Dare we lose such things, dare we break the chain that links us so absolutely to our joint history, man and animal?

We live in a time of 'bottom lines', that dreadful myopic expression, where instant profit is all that matters. In the United States today, an almost unimaginably vast producer of dairy products, almost all milk comes from one breed of cow, the Holstein. Jerseys, Guernseys, all the other breeds are rare and 'peculiar', seldom kept by anyone other than fanciers or hobbyists, and the same is true of Canada.

The genetic potential of these 'minor' breeds may soon be lost, and although they are the same species as all other domestic cattle, it would take far longer to rebuild a lost breed than mankind is likely to invest in the effort. As the Holsteins in the United States are bred to produce more and more milk a year on less and less pasture, and as the bottom line looks better and better, we can imagine the day when one enormous black and white cow will stand astride the border between Canada and the United States, pouring endless rivers of milk into the two countries. It is like science fiction. With bioengineering upon us, who can know what will happen?

All this while the still-productive breeds that made it possible are abandoned to die. For comparison, a Holstein in America (in 1971, it is even better now) produced 16,654 litres of milk in a year. A Brown Swiss produced 13,190 litres, a Guernsey 12,153 litres, a Jersey 11,097 litres and a Milking Shorthorn 8981 litres. Those are the bottom lines that decide what of our history, what of our aesthetics, what of our science can be discarded. It is more than short-sighted, it is biological vandalism.

There is another consideration, although it is the kind of eerie speculation that kept us awake at night as children, listening for a floorboard or stair to squeak. In constructing our super-cows, our super-fast horses and other now-favoured domestic animals to match, may we have inadvertently built in time warps? What if a breed (take the Holstein as an example) were to crash genetically? It is possible that any breed, particularly one that has been manipulated without pity, could become derelict after an unknown number of generations. Wild species do – why not domestic breeds? What a sad sight we would be, having thrown all the rest away. Genetic potential, gene pools, biodiversity wild or domestic – these are not things we dare treat lightly.

Books like *Rare Breeds* are vitally important for our awareness, our ability to make wise choices and to guide our own behaviour. Animals afford us enormous pleasure, they feed our minds as well as our bodies. When the animals are truly rare, there is more than pleasure to be gained from learning about them and studying their portraits. There is an urgency, a sense of how important they are to us, as they have been for a hundred and fifty centuries. They are things we must hang on to at any cost. None of that history or diversity can be spared, not if we are to maintain our identity and seek a future.

# Rare Breeds

**Whitefaced
Woodland
sheep**

During the last century, the world has seen the old patterns of livestock development of more than two millennia swept aside by the onrush of technology. Distance is no longer an obstacle to travel, and biotechnology enables fashionable breeds of livestock to penetrate every corner of the globe. The increasing uniformity of the population of animals on farms and ranches is reminiscent of the situation before many of them were domesticated, when natural selection established uniformity within each population. Modern breeds of each species are descended from only one or two subspecies of wild ancestors. Domesticated cattle are derived from the Aurochs (*Bos primigenius*), a massive, long-horned creature that stood a metre high at the shoulder and roamed throughout Europe and Asia between the 30 degree and 60 degree lines of latitude. Pigs are descended from the European wild boar (*Sus scrofa scrofa*), which was a long, lean, active, lop-eared pig, and from the wild boar of South-East Asia (*Sus scrofa vittatus*), which was fatter, matured at a younger age and had prick ears. Sheep are derived from the Asiatic moufflon (*Ovis orientalis*), and possibly also from the Urial wild sheep (*Ovis vignei*) and the big-horned Argali, also known as the Marco Polo sheep (*Ovis ammon*). Goats are descended from the Bezoar wild goat (*Capra aegagrus*); horses and ponies from *Equus ferus*; poultry from the jungle fowl of South-East Asia, and the dog from the wolf (*Canis lupus*).

Some of these wild ancestors still exist, so that it is possible to assess accurately the changes that have taken place as a result of domestication. In other cases, however, the wild ancestor is extinct. This is the case with the wild ancestor of modern breeds of horse and pony, and of wild cattle. The last Aurochs was killed in Jaktorowka Forest in north-eastern Poland in 1627.

These wild ancestors of modern farm livestock evolved gradually, moulded by the law of the survival of the fittest, their characteristics and appearance continually refined to enhance their opportunities for success in the prevailing environment.

Domestication introduced a different set of selection parameters. For example, in cattle, the size, power and aggression so necessary in the wild to the Aurochsen were undesirable characteristics to the owner who wished to exercise control over such large creatures. Thus, domesticated cattle became much smaller than their wild ancestors. Small size was also an advantage because the animals had to be fenced in so that they could be better protected from predators.

Fashion also exerted an influence at a very early stage, and characteristics that would have been a disadvantage in the wild became more frequent with domestication.

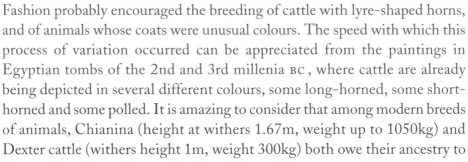

Fashion probably encouraged the breeding of cattle with lyre-shaped horns, and of animals whose coats were unusual colours. The speed with which this process of variation occurred can be appreciated from the paintings in Egyptian tombs of the 2nd and 3rd millenia BC, where cattle are already being depicted in several different colours, some long-horned, some short-horned and some polled. It is amazing to consider that among modern breeds of animals, Chianina (height at withers 1.67m, weight up to 1050kg) and Dexter cattle (withers height 1m, weight 300kg) both owe their ancestry to the Aurochs, and that the miniature flat-faced Pug and large, rangy Irish Wolfhound are both descended from the wolf.

**Exmoor pony**

Why did this amazing variety arise? In the earlier stages of domestication, it is likely that man's main objective was the security of his food supply. However, this was soon overtaken by ritualistic and aesthetic factors which persist today on the show-bench and in the show ring. The lyre-shaped horns of some breeds of cattle are reminiscent of the crescent moon, and were probably favoured as symbols within fertility cults. The impressive horns of some breeds today indicate a continuing interest in this particular characteristic. The Ankole cattle of Uganda and the Kuri cattle of Chad have enormous horns, while those of both the Texas and the English Longhorn are also particularly eye-catching. The pagan rituals of the Celts were symbolized by the colour of their cattle; red represented fertility, black, pestilence, while white represented the sun and rendered white cattle particularly valuable as sacrificial animals in the sun-worship ceremonies of the Druids.

Commercial and functional factors did play a part in the evolution and development of breeds, but at a much later stage. In some cases, this was a deliberate selection to make the animals more adaptable to their environment. The long, coarse fibres in the fleece of Blackfaced Hill sheep in the north of England and Scotland are a good protection against the cold, wet climate in those mountainous areas, while the bare neck of Transylvanian Naked-Neck fowl assists the process of heat loss in a hot continental climate. In more recent times, the selection for commercial characteristics in an artificial environment has been carried to extremes. Intensive selection programmes for pigs have produced animals with very long, lean bodies, turkeys with much enlarged breasts, and cattle and sheep with hypertrophied muscles in their hindquarters. As might be expected, selection for certain characteristics leads to the deterioration of other characteristics, and distinguishes them even

**Shetland cow**

further from their wild ancestors. Thus, some modern pigs develop weaknesses in their back and legs, while commercial turkeys are unable to mate naturally, and the calves of muscle-bound cattle frequently need to be born by Caesarean section.

The early development of breeds of livestock was complicated by massive migrations and movements of people around Europe and Asia. The original centre of domestication of livestock was probably concentrated in the Middle East, around the Fertile Crescent of the Tigris and the Euphrates rivers. It is likely that the use of domesticated livestock spread out gradually from this centre through concentric diffusion, but from the third millennium BC to AD 1000, a series of disturbances among the human populations upset the symmetrical pattern of this development. The main influences, in chronological order, during this period were the rise of the Beaker people in western Europe, the civilization of the Celts in central Europe, the migration of Germanic and Scandinavian peoples from the north, and the Asiatic invasions from the east. At an even later stage, the discovery of the Americas by the Spanish Conquistadors led to the colonization of both North and South America by livestock of Iberian origin.

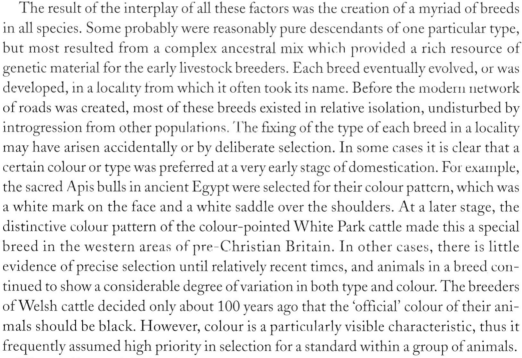

**Portland sheep**

The result of the interplay of all these factors was the creation of a myriad of breeds in all species. Some probably were reasonably pure descendants of one particular type, but most resulted from a complex ancestral mix which provided a rich resource of genetic material for the early livestock breeders. Each breed eventually evolved, or was developed, in a locality from which it often took its name. Before the modern network of roads was created, most of these breeds existed in relative isolation, undisturbed by introgression from other populations. The fixing of the type of each breed in a locality may have arisen accidentally or by deliberate selection. In some cases it is clear that a certain colour or type was preferred at a very early stage of domestication. For example, the sacred Apis bulls in ancient Egypt were selected for their colour pattern, which was a white mark on the face and a white saddle over the shoulders. At a later stage, the distinctive colour pattern of the colour-pointed White Park cattle made this a special breed in the western areas of pre-Christian Britain. In other cases, there is little evidence of precise selection until relatively recent times, and animals in a breed continued to show a considerable degree of variation in both type and colour. The breeders of Welsh cattle decided only about 100 years ago that the 'official' colour of their animals should be black. However, colour is a particularly visible characteristic, thus it frequently assumed high priority in selection for a standard within a group of animals.

The small size of the locality occupied by each breed can be illustrated by the sheep breeds in the Dales of Yorkshire in England. Each Dale is only a few square miles in area, yet each boasts its own breed – Teeswater, Swaledale, Wensleydale, et cetera. Each breed was adapted to the local climate and system of management, its position secured by its association with the area and the loyalty or conservatism of its owners through succeeding generations. Such a state of affairs could not persist indefinitely. Increasing industrialization disturbed the existing social structure, more in some cases than others. There was a general movement of people from rural areas to towns and

**British Lop pig**

cities. The acceptance of old systems and practices could no longer be taken for granted. This led inevitably to the erosion of the territory of some breeds, and in many cases progressed to ultimate and irretrievable loss. Some breeds disappeared quite rapidly as a result of direct breed substitution. Pig breeds proved particularly susceptible to extinction by this method. For example, in northern Spain in 1955, the Chato Vitoriano had a population of more than 80,000 sows; today it is extinct. Other breeds disappeared less dramatically as a result of crossbreeding. Males of popular fashionable breeds are imported and mated to the local females through succeeding generations. After only a few generations, the genome, or complete set of chromosomes, of the original indigenous population has been diluted to negligible proportions.

The scale of loss has been enormous. In western Europe, at the beginning of the twentieth century, there were about 230 native breeds of cattle. By 1988, only about 30 of these breeds were secure; 70 had become extinct; and 53 were in an endangered state; while the remainder were minority breeds, not immediately endangered but far from secure. In Great Britain alone, 26 breeds of large livestock have become extinct during the present century. The loss of native pig breeds in Europe has been even more severe. Forty years ago, 70 breeds existed. Now only 24 remain and several of those are seriously endangered.

The list of extinct breeds evokes poignant memories. Suffolk Dun cattle were an outstanding dairy breed. The Lincolnshire Curly Coat pig was a distinctive hairy animal, whose only genetic legacy is its contribution to the ancestry of the modern American breed, the Chester White. Cushendale, Long Mynd and Goonhilly ponies have romantic local associations. France has lost seven cattle breeds, including the Borderlaise, Semeline and Mezenc. Some of the genetic material may be conserved in Canada, where the Canadienne breed is derived from earlier native breeds of northwest France. Similarly, several Iberian pig breeds are extinct in their native country, but their influence can still be seen in some relic populations in the Americas. Some breeds claim to have survived, but have done so in name only. Widespread crossbreeding can completely change the character of a population, but its original name will sometimes still persist. Thus the Hanoverian working horse in Germany, as a result of genetic change, is now a performance sport horse. In other cases, a breed has become extinct, but the type has been reconstructed by mixing appropriate breeds and the former name has been adopted. The Bayeux pig in France and the Oxford Sandy and Black pig in Britain both became extinct in the early 1970s and both have been 'revived', although the new population owes no part of its ancestry to the animals that formerly carried the same name. There have been equally futile attempts to reconstruct wild Aurochsen cattle and the Tarpan horse.

The majority of genuine native breeds that have survived are seriously threatened, and many owe their survival to the strong emergence of the genetic conservation movement during the last two or three decades. 'Rare Breeds' organizations now exist in many countries, under the global coordination of the umbrella organization, 'Rare

Breeds International'. The oldest national organization is the Rare Breeds Survival Trust in Britain which started as a working party in 1968 and was established formally in 1973. In the United States there is the American Livestock Breeds Conservancy, which was founded in 1977. Since then similar organizations have been founded in many other countries. There is a growing realization of the importance of saving those breeds that remain.

In Europe, the greatest variety of breeds was found in the United Kingdom, France, Germany and Italy. There have been the greatest losses in these countries, but they still retain many native breeds. In the United Kingdom, the recognized breeds of large livestock on the Priority and Minority Lists of the Rare Breeds Survival Trust total 54 – 13 cattle, 24 sheep, 2 goats, 7 pigs and 8 horse or pony breeds. In Germany there are 40 endangered breeds (13 cattle, 11 sheep, 4 goats, 3 pigs and 9 horse or pony breeds). Information from several countries is not always complete, and there still remains the danger of a breed becoming extinct, even in the midst of a conservation-oriented society.

The value of these breeds can easily be underestimated. They should not be dismissed as irrelevant relics of a bygone era, or as primitive and obsolete curiosities in a livestock industry shaped by high technology. It is increasingly being realized that much of the value of the old breeds resides in the fact that they have bypassed the intensive selection and extreme development that has determined the character of popular breeds in recent decades.

**Girgentana goat**

The justification for conserving endangered breeds of livestock is based firmly on their historical relevance and their contribution to the heritage of their country of origin. Soay sheep, which were confined to the St Kilda group of islands in the Outer Hebrides until 1930, probably arrived in northern Europe more than 4,000 years ago, and closely resemble their wild ancestor, the Asiatic moufflon. They are small and active, brown and short-tailed. Their behaviour is more typical of wild sheep than of their domesticated relatives. Many of the primitive breeds of sheep in northern Europe belong to the short-tailed group. They include the Romanov from Russia, the Gotland from Sweden, the Icelandic, and the Shetland and North Ronaldsay from the archipelagos at the northern fringe of the British Isles.

The Berrenda, Retinta and Mostrenca cattle of Andalusia, and the White Park cattle of the British Isles, probably enjoy a history as ancient as the Soay sheep. Their place in history is ensured by their respective roles as ancestors of the Texas Longhorn and as the sacrificial cattle of the Druids. The White Park has been a special breed at several stages of history. It was mentioned in the oral folk-stories of pre-Christian Ireland, and figured prominently in the Laws of the Welsh Prince, Hywel Dda, in the tenth century. It was enclosed in the hunting chases of the Plantagenet kings, and was a favourite subject of famous artists such as Sir Edwin Landseer.

Other breeds are also worthy of mention. The Exmoor pony is perhaps the most ancient equine breed in Europe. Five-toed Dorking poultry were mentioned by the agricultural commentator Columella at the time of the Roman invasion of Britain.

**Silver Sussex hen**

The original Merino sheep, the basis of the wool industries in Australia and New Zealand, are still found in small numbers in their native haunts in southern Spain, while an historic off shoot, the Merino de Rambouillet, is conserved near Paris. Many of the ancient breeds are notable for their aesthetic appeal, particularly with regard to their spectacular horns and unusual colours. The horns of English Longhorn and Texas Longhorn cattle assume a variety of unusual styles and shapes, but even they are not as curious as the proliferation of horns possessed by some breeds of sheep. Once, sheep breeds from regions as far apart as North Africa and Iberia, the islands around the British Isles and the Americas, had a multi-horned characteristic which is still found in the Hebridean, Manx Loghtan, Jacob and Navajo-Churro sheep. Some colour patterns are also widespread. A white belt has been sported by Belted Galloway, Bolian Gwynion, Sheeted Somerset, Lakenvelder, Brown Swiss and Dutch Belted cattle, and Cinta Senese, Angeln Sattelschwein, Schwabisch-Hallisches, British Saddleback and Hampshire pigs. Variety of colour in a breed has always been contrary to the traditional philosophy of uniformity since breed standards were established, but it has been an essential ingredient of the Shetland Islands' woollen industry.

A breed which is closely related to Shetland sheep demonstrates the second justification for the conservation of rare breeds. North Ronaldsay sheep are adapted to a most unusual system of management on their native island in the Orkney archipelago. For most of the year, they are excluded from the grassland areas by a tall wall which completely encircles the island. They exist on an exclusive diet of seaweed, and this has caused changes in their physiology and metabolism which are of great scientific interest. They are extremely susceptible to copper toxicity, but can tolerate high levels of urea and potassium. Another exciting discovery is that the muscle tissue and lipids of some ancient breeds, such as Hebridean sheep and White Park cattle, have a significantly lower level of cholesterol than popular breeds. This valuable characteristic may be shared by old breeds of poultry, and is likely to be enhanced by the adaption of these breeds to extensive systems of management. A potentially beneficial effect on human health may not be far in the future.

Some endangered breeds have already demonstrated that their loss would deprive the livestock industry of valuable genetic material. Fashion has played a powerful role in determining the popularity of each breed, and has often obscured their true value. It has been an important function of the 'rare breeds' organizations in each country to identify the special characteristics of endangered breeds, and to define the systems of management for which they are best suited. These characteristics fall into three main categories, namely their yield of high-quality products, their value in ecological projects of environmental value, and their suitability for systems of management which pay particular regard to animal welfare. These factors are assuming increasing importance in contemporary society. Breeds that thrive in extensive, rather than intensive, systems of management and on low-energy feed are more in sympathy with recent trends than are those which require controlled environments and high-energy, concentrated feed. Trials carried out in Germany with rare pig breeds have confirmed their suitability for outdoor extensive systems, and shown the different effect of each breed on the botanical composition of their paddocks. Trials in England have similarly demonstrated the superiority of Hebridean sheep in controlling encroaching scrub on common land and tough weeds on sand dunes. These qualities, allied to the superior flavour, texture and colour of their meat, are available only because the breeds have been conserved.

With some breeds, it is less easy to justify their conservation on the basis of any of the factors detailed above. However, support for their survival is equally deserved. Bagot goats, Ushant sheep, Bentheimer and Limousin pigs, Gloucester and Murnau Werdenfelser cattle have little to recommend them if they are judged solely on their possible contribution to recognized systems of livestock production. However, no-one can predict what the future holds. Markets may change, fashions will change, and a breed which is severely endangered today may possess a quality that is of vital importance in the future. All endangered breeds need to be conserved as an insurance against unknown circumstances. They are part of a heritage that must be passed down to future generations in an unpredictable world. They may find a role as pure breeds, or they may be used in the creation of new breeds which bring a wider dimension to the ongoing association of mankind and domesticated livestock. There are many precedents for this. The seriously endangered Norfolk Horn sheep was an ancestor of the popular and success-ful Suffolk; the previously rare Lleyn was used in the development of the high-perfor-mance British Milksheep; Suffolk Dun cattle (now extinct) were ancestors of the rare Red Poll, which in turn was used in the creation of the Jamaica Red; while the Chester White pig contains the influence of two extinct breeds, the Cumberland and the Lincolnshire Curly Coat. All the same, a partial contribution to a modern breed is a poor substitute for survival.

**White Croad Langshan cock**

# Pigs

Modern pig breeds are derived mainly from a mixture of European
and Asiatic wild ancestors, whose contrasting characteristics can be identified
in varying proportions in modern breeds.
The pig industry in the developed world has been fashioned during the
twentieth century by breeding selection for bacon pigs,
reared in intensive conditions, often in controlled environments.
This trend has now been reversed, and once again the valuable qualities of
several endangered breeds of pig are being more fully appreciated, especially as
these breeds are better adapted to systems of management which pay high
regard to animal welfare and to the natural environment.

## Tamworth

The origin of the red colour of the
Tamworth is a matter of some mystery.
It is rumoured that it was derived from
an animal known as the Axford pig,
imported into Britain from Barbados
in the mid-nineteenth century, and that
the breed was developed in the Midlands
by Sir Robert Peel (1788–1850), the
politician and Prime Minister. Although
in Britain the Tamworth is now seriously
endangered, in previous times it was
exported to many other parts of the world,
where it showed itself to be remarkably
adaptable to several different climates.

*above*
**Tamworth**
Recently, some Tamworths have been re-imported to the United Kingdom from Australia, and have re-established three sire lines – Jasper, Glen and Royal Standard – which have been very successful. This eight-month-old gilt, Berkswell Lucky Lass 131, is from one of the oldest and most prestigious herds of the breed, and is the daughter of a boar descended from the original imported Jasper.

*right*
**British Lop**
The British Lop (originally the National Long White Lop-Eared) is an old breed that has always been restricted to particular areas, mainly in the south-west tip of England. It is probably related to similar breeds found around the north-western fringes of Europe, namely the Welsh, and the Landrace pig breeds of Scandinavia. It may also be related to the Normande pigs of north-western France. Because of its isolated location, the British Lop has always been an endangered breed, but sadly it has been unable to take advantage of this as a rare breed in farm parks because its appearance and colour are seen as lacking in interest.

*overleaf*
**Gloucestershire Old Spots**
This sow and her litter of piglets have their home at the Temple Newsam Estate near Leeds, in Yorkshire – one of the most important Approved Centres within the programme established by the Rare Breeds Survival Trust.

*above*

**Gloucestershire Old Spots**

The native pig of Gloucestershire developed in a special environment in the Berkeley Vale. It was at one time known as the Orchard pig, because it was used to scavenge windfall apples. It was also fed on whey, a by-product of the local dairy industry. It is now known as the Gloucestershire Old Spots, but many pigs scarcely earn that title as they have only the smallest amount of black on their body. Previously, the pigs were much more heavily marked with several black spots and blotches.

*right*

**Gloucestershire Old Spots**

The Gloucestershire Old Spots is noted as a careful and conscientious mother. She also usually produces a large litter of piglets – Ainsley Josephine 810 had ten litter mates.

**Blonde Mangalitza**

Hungary possesses a large number of fascinating old breeds of livestock, many of which are now seriously endangered. The Mangalitza pig is a most unusual animal as it grows a hairy 'fleece', akin to that of a sheep. The only other pig breed noted for having a long coat was the now extinct Lincolnshire Curly Coat in England. The Mangalitza was formerly bred as a lard pig, and the animals were large and rotund. It was the drop in demand for lard that led to the decline of the breed.

**Bentheimer**

The Bentheimer is a lop-eared, spotted pig, also known as the Schwarz-Weisses or Buntes Schwein. It benefits from a government subsidy, paid for each purebred litter produced. This support is vital, as the breed survives only in a very small population in a few herds, and does not compare favourably with other breeds for performance characteristics. Its genetic integrity has also been diluted from time to time by crossing with other German and British breeds. However, it has now been established as a useful breed for extensive systems of management. Unlike some other breeds, it tends to remove all the grass cover from its paddocks, which consequently often become dominated by docks (*Rumex* species).

### British Saddleback

The British Saddleback breed was established in 1967 as a result of the amalgamation of the Essex and Wessex breeds. These two widely separated populations differed in type, the Essex having been strongly influenced by imported Neapolitan pigs, while the Wessex was much more typical of the old-fashioned British type. However, they shared a common colour pattern, being black with a white belt which encircled the body at the shoulders. The two types are now thoroughly and inextricably intermixed. The British Saddleback is very well adapted to outdoor systems of management, having a quiet temperament and being an excellent grazer. It is also a very good maternal breed, producing large litters of fast-growing piglets.

The origin of the colour pattern of saddleback pigs is uncertain, but was first recorded in Tuscany where a similarly marked, equally endangered breed, the Cinta Senese, is still found. As well as the British Saddleback, the Wessex was also an ancestor of the Hampshire, a saddleback breed found in North America.

**Berkshire**

In earlier times, the local pig of Berkshire, Buckinghamshire and Oxfordshire was a large, rangy animal, red-brown in colour, with extensive black markings. It was changed from the late eighteenth century onwards by crossing with imported pigs of Asiatic origin. These animals (which arrived via Italy, where they were known as the Neapolitan), were small, rotund and black. The modern Berkshire has inherited many of the characteristics of these Asiatic ancestors, being an early maturing breed with prick ears. It is black with six white points, namely its feet, the tip of its tail and its snout. In earlier times it was exported to other parts of the world, particularly North America and Australasia, and in 1976 an Australian boar, Lynjoleen Ambassador 1183, was re-imported to the United Kingdom and exerted a very beneficial effect on the breed. More re-importations of Berkshire pigs from Australia are planned during the 1990s.

*above*

## Rotbunte

Most saddleback breeds of pig are black in colour.
The exception is the Rotbunte, which is red. It is
an offshoot of the Angeln Sattelschwein, and is
also known as the Husumer, after the locality in
northern Germany where it originated. Its grazing
habit favours the growth of *Juncus* species of rushes,
which dominate in the paddocks where it is kept.

*left*

## Angeln Sattelschwein

The Angeln Sattelschwein was established in the
mid-nineteenth century as a result of crosses
between the British Saddleback and local German
Landrace pigs. It became established in Schleswig-
Holstein as a separate and distinct breed, although
there has recently been some further limited
introgression. It is a very fecund breed, and a sow
will produce 21 or 22 piglets per annum. It was
highly valued for this quality, and by the middle of
the twentieth century, comprised about one-seventh
of the total pig population of Germany. However,
by the mid-1980s the population had fallen to a
negligible size and the breed was seriously
endangered. It is well adapted to outdoor systems
of management and is likely to see an upturn in its
fortunes as breeders turn away from more intensive
systems of production.

*left*

**Large Black**

This Large Black is from the Temple Newsam Estate near Leeds in Yorkshire, which maintains a comprehensive selection of endangered British breeds of pig. The Large Black is a very docile breed, possibly because its large, drooping ears obscure its vision.

*above*

**Large Black**

The Large Black resulted from the amalgamation of black pigs from south-west England with those from East Anglia. The pigs from East Anglia, mainly Essex, were strongly influenced by importations from China in the late eighteenth century, while those from Devon and Cornwall were probably much more closely related to pigs on the mainland of Europe, particularly in France. It is remarkably fecund: this eight-month-old boar, Bassingbourn Attempt IV, was one of a litter of thirteen piglets.

*above*

**Gascon**

Conservation programmes for the Gascon pig have now been set up by the Chambre Régionale de Midi-Pyrénées, in conjunction with l'École Nationale Vétérinaire de Toulouse and l'Institut du Porc.

*left*

**Gascon**

A few old, traditional breeds of pig have survived in the more mountainous and remote regions of France. In the mid-Pyrenean region there is a particularly endangered breed, the Gascon, which is probably the most ancient breed of pig in France. Despite its endangered status, it has many valuable characteristics. Like most old-fashioned breeds, it is prone to becoming very fat, but it is vigorous, hardy, thrifty and can tolerate hot climates. The sows are prolific and have a good supply of milk for their litters.

## Middle White

Middle Whites are a speciality pork breed, and have suffered as a result of market trends which have favoured bacon pigs. The breed derives originally from crosses made in Yorkshire in the mid-nineteenth century between the Large White and the now extinct Small White, and still betrays considerable evidence of its Asiatic ancestor, *Sus scrofa vittatus*, the South-East Asian wild boar. In Japan, the breed is held in such high regard that a memorial has been erected to three Middle White boars – Newton Firethorn, Pendley Bugle Boy and Pendley Drummer Boy IV.

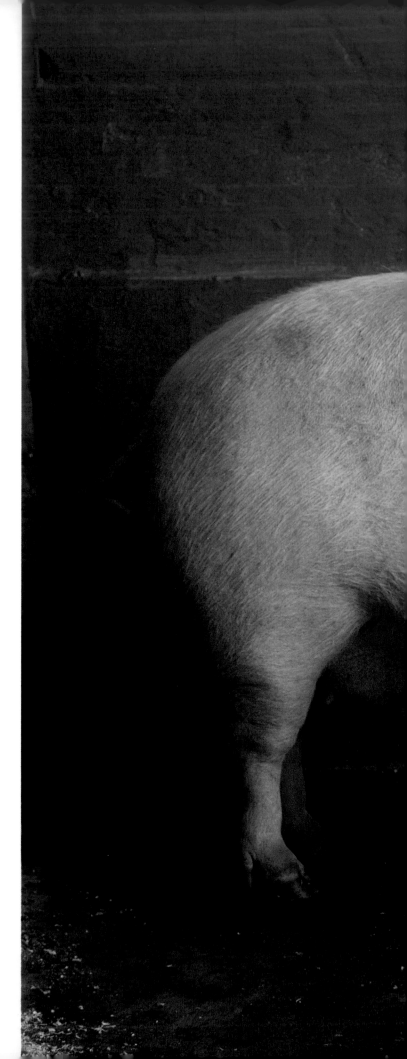

*left*
**Middle White**
In the United Kingdom, pigs derive their name from their parent, with males adopting the name of their sire and females the name of their dam. Thus Smethurst Purity, the nine-month-old Middle White gilt or young sow pictured here, is a daughter of Billington Purity III. Her sire was Churchmews Rajah.

*above*
**Middle White**
The Middle White is one of the most seriously endangered breeds of pig in the United Kingdom. Although very few animals now exist, it was extremely popular in the first half of the twentieth century, when it attracted considerable attention from breeders in the Far East and many pigs were exported, especially to Japan. This interest has continued to some degree, and further exports were made to Japan in 1987.

# Cattle

Although cattle are now found in all parts of the globe,
their ancestor, the Aurochs, was found in a relatively restricted area of Europe,
western Asia and the northern fringe of Africa.
A great variety of breeds has been derived from this single source,
varying in size, shape, colour and function; some with horns, some polled,
some for milk and some for meat production.
However, the original religious and ritualistic reasons for domesticating cattle,
and their early use as draught-animals, have now largely disappeared.

## British White

British White cattle were first recorded at Whalley Abbey in Lancashire in the early seventeenth century. From there, they spread southwards into Cheshire and eventually into East Anglia, where the major part of the breed has been concentrated for more than a hundred years. The Wimpole Herd of British White cattle is situated in this region and six-year-old Leah is a prize-winning cow from the herd.

Until the middle of the twentieth century, the British White was a dairy breed, but it has gradually been replaced by more specialist, high-performance breeds, such as the Friesian and the Holstein. During the past 40 years, it has changed in type and is now a beef breed, selected for rapid growth rate. Cattle descended from the British White are now found in Australia and North America.

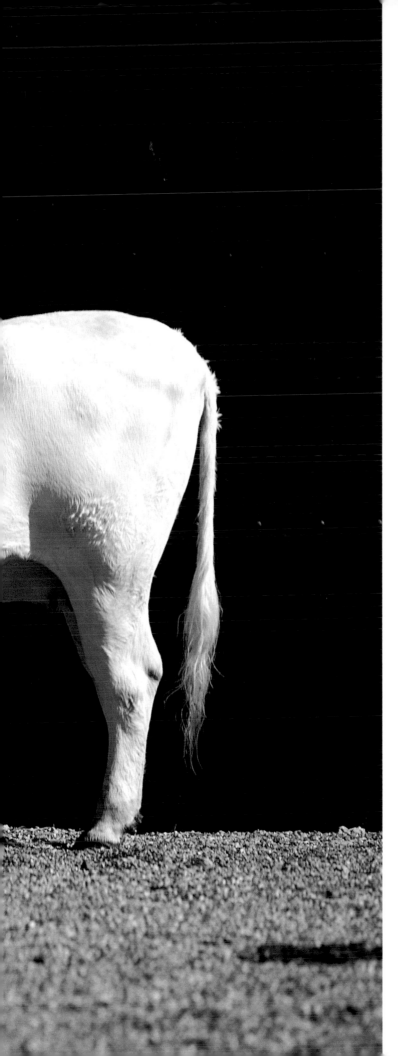

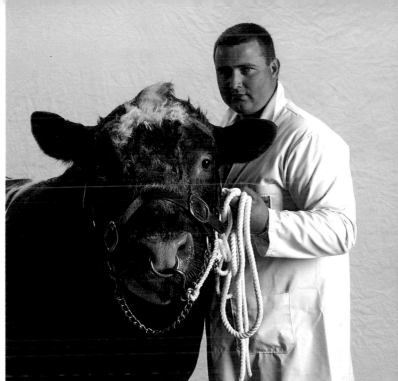

**Beef Shorthorn**

Shorthorn cattle are all descended from the old Teeswater group of north-east England, and probably, originally, were of Dutch origin. The Shorthorn breed was first developed and popularized by the Colling brothers, who farmed in Teesdale in the last quarter of the eighteenth century, and practised systems of inbreeding as a result of their visit to Robert Bakewell, the distinguished Longhorn breeder. Their famous bull, Comet, which was highly inbred, sold at the Ketton Sale in 1810 for the then amazing sum of 1,000 guineas. The Shorthorn subsequently split into different types, and the Beef Shorthorn became a Scottish breed. From there, it was exported to improve the native cattle of the prairies of North America, the pampas of South America and the plains of Australia. Bromborough Ben Hur, a two-year-old bull, is a light roan colour, but animals of this breed may also be red, white or red and white.

*left*
**British White**

Wimpole Leah. She shows the typical colour pattern of the breed, which is white with black points, sometimes with black spots on the neck and shoulders and black pigmentation of the skin.

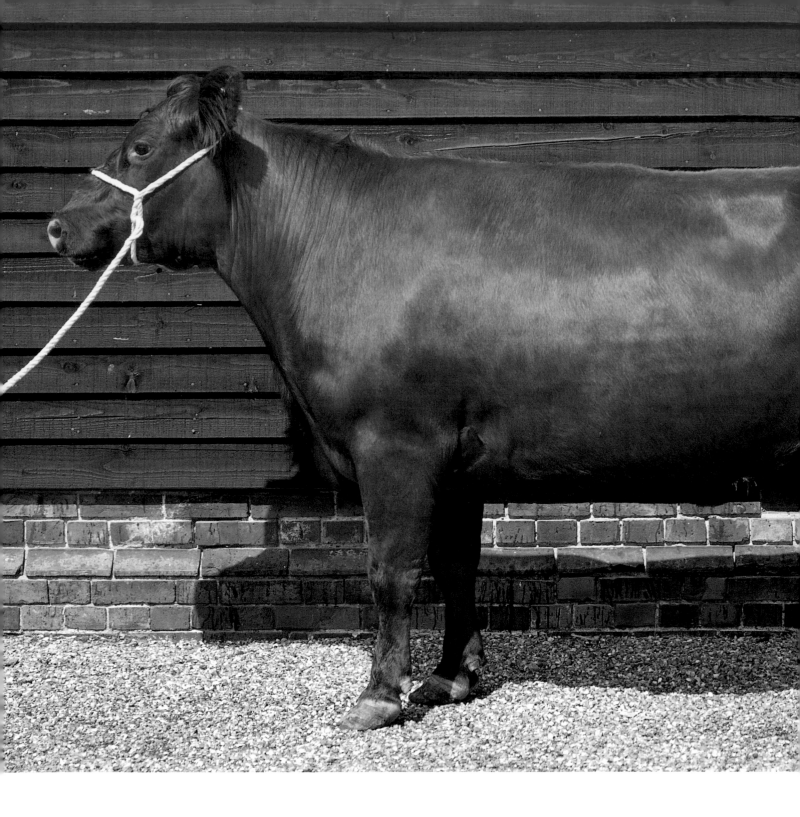

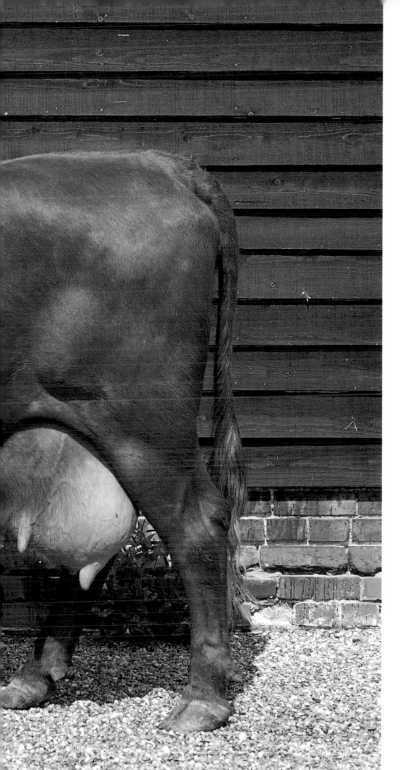

*above*
## Red Poll

Although most pedigree herds are privately owned, some important herds are maintained by organizations and corporate bodies. Cheshire County Council breed a leading herd of Red Poll cattle at Tatton Park, and their two-and-a-half-year-old bull, Tatton Red Eric, was Breed Champion at the Royal Show and Reserve Inter Breed Champion at the Rare Breeds Show & Sale in 1993. The Red Poll was formed by the amalgamation of two breeds, both of which are now extinct – the horned Red Norfolk and the high-milk-yielding Suffolk Dun. The Red Poll inherited the colour of the Red Norfolk and the polledness of the Suffolk Dun, and combines their qualities of milk and beef production as a dual-purpose breed.

*left*
## Red Poll

During the second half of the twentieth century, there has been increasing specialization in British livestock farming. In particular, breeds of cattle have been selected either for milk or for beef production. Consequently, old draught breeds or dual-purpose breeds such as the Red Poll have become less popular, and in many cases have been brought close to extinction. There is evidence that once again the cycle of fashion is turning, and that cows such as Capps Chimp will help to restore their fortunes.

*above*

**Shetland**

Since the mid-1970s, a number of Shetland cattle have been moved from their native islands to the mainland of Britain, and Shetlands are now found in several different herds in the United Kingdom. Croxteth Alexandra, a two-and-a-half-year-old heifer, comes from a farm park owned by Liverpool City Council and located within the city boundaries.

Shetland cattle become extremely attached to their keepers, and on the Shetland crofts this was usually the farmer's wife. The attachment was so strong that cows frequently refused to accept a new owner unless a portion of their previous keeper's clothing accompanied them. This was known as a 'clout', and thus Shetland cattle also became known as 'cloutie coos'.

*right*

**Shetland**

The crofters on the Shetland Islands required a very specific type of animal: hardy, thrifty and small in size, as a large animal would find it difficult to survive in such inhospitable terrain. It also needed to supply the crofters with a variety of products, from power as a draught-animal to milk and meat. Thus the Shetland is an extremely functional animal, with few concessions made to appearance or style. It is one of the smallest breeds of cattle in Britain and is usually mainly black in colour, although 70 or 80 years ago some animals were dun while others had a lighter stripe down the back and a lighter ring of hair around the muzzle.

*above*
**Irish Moiled**

Templeson Serin, a two year old bull, seen here with Mr David Bradley, who runs the Leeds City Council rare breeds farm at Temple Newsam in Yorkshire. The name 'moiled' has an Irish derivation, and indicates a mound shaped like the top of the head of a polled animal. The Irish Moiled has the typical ring-straked colour pattern, also seen in Pusterthaler and Longhorn cattle, of a white line down the back and a white tail, but the amount of colour varies greatly from almost totally white to only a minimally ring-straked pattern.

*left*
**Irish Moiled**

The Irish Moiled is one of the most seriously endangered breeds of cattle in the British Isles. Until recently, it was restricted entirely to Northern Ireland and its existence was threatened by crossbreeding with Finnish, Shorthorn and Lincoln Red crosses. Several new herds have now been established in England and Argory Adeline, seen here with her month-old bull calf Fergus, is a foundation cow of the Wimpole herd near Cambridge.

*above*

**Kerry**

The Kerry is probably an ancient breed, and has possible associations with the Celts. Its small size is a result of it having adapted to the low fertility of the countryside of south-west Ireland, its region of origin. Most herds are still found in this area, around Killarney, but small groups have also been exported to England and Canada. It is a light-framed, graceful dairy breed, with up-tilted horns and pure black in colour. Although not a high-milk-yielder, its importance lies in the fact that it can produce milk in localities where most other breeds would find it difficult even to survive.

**Gloucester**

Gloucester cattle are very localized, being limited almost entirely to their county of origin. Their development and success have been prevented by other more popular breeds, such as the Shorthorn in the nineteenth, and the Friesian during the twentieth century. These have also been crossed with it, so the modern Gloucester is a mixture of these plus the original breed. It has a modest milk yield, and has changed from a dairy to a dual-purpose breed. It is mostly found in suckler herds, rearing its own calves.

**Pusterthaler Sprinzen**

The Pusterthaler has two alternative names which describe its colour pattern. One variety is called Schecken, which denotes a spotted pattern, and the other is Sprinzen, which is translated as 'sprinkled'. The latter have only coloured points and a few spots of colour on the neck, while the former are colour-sided in a pattern found in breeds in several countries, including the Vosgienne in France, the Longhorn in England and the Irish Moiled in Ireland.

Cattle

*above*

**Belted Galloway**

Animals which live in exposed areas or regions with a harsh climate develop a long, thick, protective coat. The Belted Galloway has a dense, double-layered coat, the inner layer being thick and close, to protect it against penetrating cold winds, while the longer outer coat sheds the rain. There are several other colour varieties of the Galloway breed, including the Black, Dun and White. The origin of its colour pattern is most probably to be found in Holland, where a native breed, the Lakenvelder (literally 'White Sheet'), shows a similar pattern. The black coat of this animal appears to be tinged with brown, but this shows only where the hair has been sun-bleached and weather-beaten.

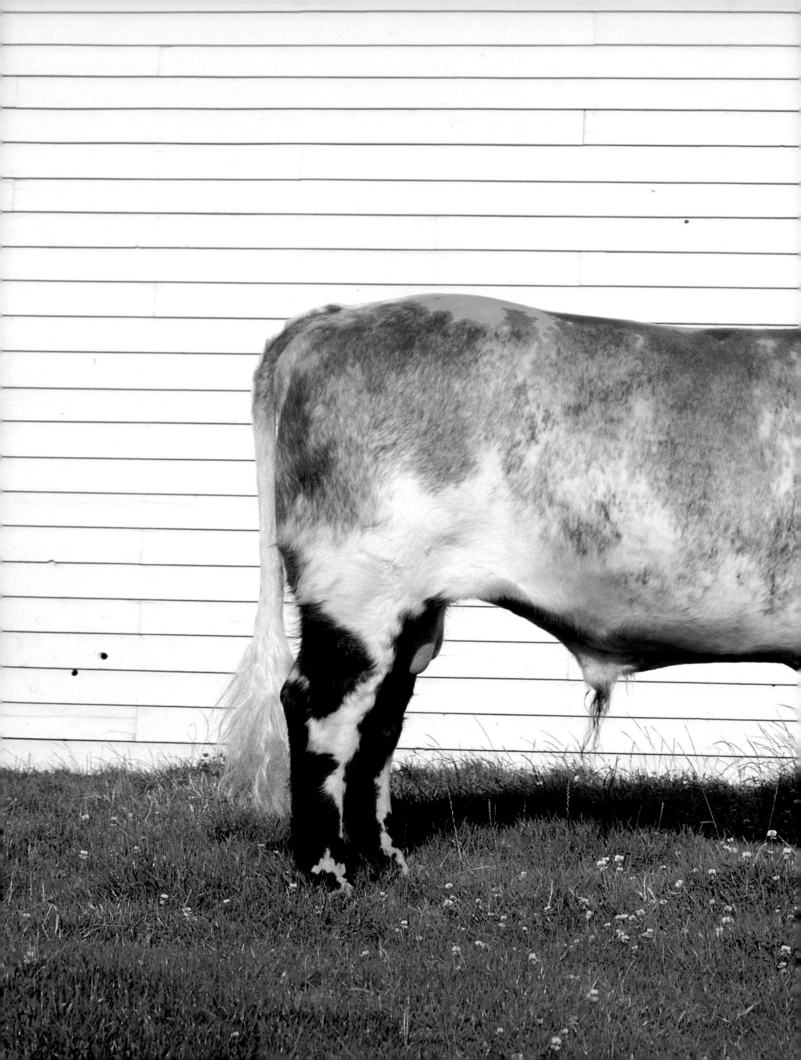

*above*

**Highland**

Highland or Kyloe cattle. Their alternative name is derived from the practise of droving the animals from the Western Isles to the mainland of Scotland by swimming them over the straits or kyles separating the areas of land.

*right*

**Highland**

The picturesque appearance of Highland cattle belies their hardy constitution. They are a favourite subject for photographers and artists, and add a glamorous touch to the mountainous regions of Scotland. Their long, thick coat and thrifty nature have enabled them to survive outdoors in the inhospitable conditions of their native region.

*previous pages*

**Beef Shorthorn**

Chapelton Eclipse, a Shorthorn bull. Changing fashions in recent years have demanded that cattle should be larger, with rapid growth rates. The Beef Shorthorn, by contrast, had been bred for a special-ized export market, which required small size and a very compact frame. In order to meet the changed requirements of the market, crossbreeding pro-grammes with a French breed, the Maine Anjou, were undertaken, and both Bromborough Ben Hur (see page 43) and Chapelton Eclipse contain an infusion from this breed.

*left*
**White Park**

The White Park is perhaps the most ancient breed of cattle in the British Isles. There are records of cattle of this type in pre-Christian Ireland, where they were associated with the sun worship of the Celts. It is highly probable that they were the sacrificial cattle of the Druids. More than a thousand years ago, White Park cattle were mentioned in the tenth-century Welsh Laws of Hywel Dda, who ruled from Dinefwr Castle. The Dynevor (modern spelling) herd still exists, and Dynevor Jock was the double grand-sire of the dam of Ash Kirsten, an eight-year-old cow from the Wimpole herd. Despite its wild ancestry, the White Park is now a very docile breed, but Kirsten is nonetheless alert in defence of her calf, which was born in 1993 while she was being exhibited at the Essex Show.

*above*
**Longhorn**

When a breed is endangered, it must be promoted. Four-year-old Bollin Jill is a frequent visitor to the show ring, and in 1993 was a winner at the Cheshire Show. Increasing the population of a rare breed is also vitally important, and modern technology can be of assistance in achieving this. For example, the development of embryo collection has given threatened breeds a far greater opportunity to survive, and one flush of eggs from Bollin Jill has resulted in eight embryos being stored for future use.

*previous pages*

**Longhorn**

Longhorn cattle probably originated in the Craven district of Yorkshire, and were developed there and in Cumbria. The breed sprang to fame due to the work of Robert Bakewell of Dishley Grange in Leicestershire. He changed the character of the Longhorn from an old triple-purpose breed to a pure beef breed, which met the nutritional needs of workers in the Industrial Revolution. The Longhorn became extremely popular, but its decline came about due to its spectacular horns, which made it difficult to house safely.

*above*
**Auroise**
An Auroise calf, displaying the typical colour pattern of many cattle native to central France and northern Spain, with a lighter ring of hair or 'halo' round the muzzle.

*left*
**Auroise**
There are several endangered breeds inhabiting the Pyrenean region, but one of the most seriously endangered is the Auroise breed of cattle. In 1993 only 19 herds, containing a total of 54 cows, remained. The breed is also known as the Aurea et Girons, or the Casta. Its primary function had been as a draught-animal, and in former times it was used for transporting felled timber from wooded areas. It has also been used for milk production and in the nineteenth century provided milk for the city of Toulouse. A number of the cattle are now kept in hobby herds. However, it remains a small, hardy, outdoor breed.

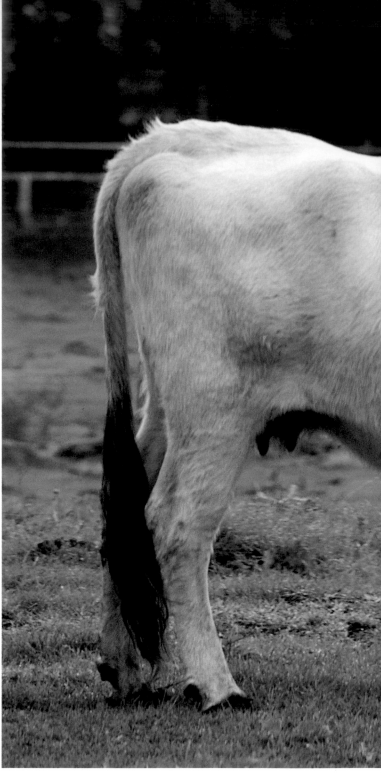

*above*
**Grey Steppe**

Grey Steppe bulls usually have a darker coloured body than the cows, as shown by this bull. His lighter coloured face and dark eye patches are also typical. The large, upright horns are important in battles between the animals to establish dominance within the herd.

*right*
**Grey Steppe**

Hungary has a long history of genetic conservation programmes, and Grey Steppe cattle have become an integral part of a wider ecological conservation programme on the flat steppes of the Puszta in eastern Hungary. Large groups of the cattle are herded there by horsemen in traditional costumes and, at some times of the year, separate groups of 30 or more mature bulls can be found in impressive array. Grey Steppe cattle are lean and long-legged, with a light frame, in order to enable them to travel over the Puszta, as did their nomadic ancestors. Their horns are usually upright and lyre-shaped, the horns of this cow not being particularly typical, but a variety of different horn styles exist within the breed.

*above*

**Chillingham**

There are very few herds of feral cattle in Great Britain. Perhaps the best known is the Chillingham herd of white cattle in Northumberland. The herd is now restricted to a 350-acre park, and consists of about 50 animals. They receive only the barest amount of management and are not provided with any shelter or housing. This rain-soaked calf shows that even feral stock do not enjoy inclement weather.

*right*

**Chillingham**

The Chillingham has the same origin as modern White Park cattle, but they have been separated for more than 700 years and are now entirely different in type. Their lean and primitive frame permits faster movement than that of domesticated cattle. An adult Chillingham cow will weigh only about 280kgs, compared with a White Park cow of 630kgs.

Chillingham bulls grow curly hair on their head and neck, and the growth of longer hair helps to protect them in a wet climate. They have dark noses and red ears, but the colour pattern is not as distinct as that found in White Park cattle, which have more strongly marked black points.

# Sheep and Goats

Sheep and goats were first domesticated in the Middle East.
Their ancestors were adapted to living in rocky upland areas, in contrast
to cattle, which were developed in areas of fertile grassland.
Thus, sheep and goats have been less easy to adapt to developed agricultural
systems, and their continuing susceptibility to problems
such as respiratory complaints and footrot are a legacy of this.
Sheep have now spread to all parts of the world
and have been selected for many different purposes. They vary from breeds
which produce an abundance of fine wool to those which have only a short,
hairy coat, while in many parts of the world they are still valued
mainly for their production of milk, which was probably their earliest
agricultural function.

**Manx Loghtan**

A hundred years ago the native sheep on the Isle of Man were small, primitive, active and varied in colour. Around the turn of the century the breeder Caesar Bacon established a selection programme and fixed the brown colour in the breed which then gave rise to its name. 'Loghtan' is derived from the Manx words *lugh*, meaning 'mouse' and *dhoan*, meaning 'brown'. Sheep have been exported to the mainland of Britain to establish new flocks, but some semi-feral flocks still remain on the island.

Manx Loghtan sheep sometimes have a multi-horned characteristic, and can grow more than one pair of horns. Sheep with this tendency are found in different parts of the world, but there appear to have been two main areas from which they originated. Sheep from North Africa are probably the ancestors of multi-horned sheep in Iberia and subsequently in the Americas, while another group, to which the Manx Loghtan belongs, is found in the north-eastern areas of Europe.

*above*
## Whitefaced Woodland

Almost all the hill breeds of sheep that inhabit the Pennines in the North of England are black-faced. The main exception is the Whitefaced Woodland, which originates in the area of the Snake Pass in Yorkshire, on the boundaries of Cheshire and Derbyshire. An alternative name for the breed is the Penistone, after a local market town in Yorkshire, where classes for the breed have been held at the annual fair since 1699. The white face and pink nose of the Whitefaced Woodland are distinctive features, as are the horns, which have marked ridges. In some cases, the horns grow into the cheeks and must be trimmed back in older animals.

*left*
## Norfolk Horn

Most breeds of livestock experience fluctuating fortunes, contrasting success with unpopularity, but a few breeds have been seriously threatened for an extended period. More than two hundred years ago, it was recorded that the Norfolk Horn was in danger of extinction, and it continues in much the same state at the present time, having only been saved by the efforts of one man, John D. Sayer. Although it bears a superficial resemblance to the horned black-faced breeds of the Pennines, its short, tight wool is specially adapted to the cold and windy, but relatively dry, climate of its native Breckland (East Anglian heathland). In that habitat, its long legs and active nature were very necessary to obtain sufficient nutrients from the sparse grazing.

Sheep and Goats

## Hill Radnor

There are many breeds and varieties of sheep in the mountains and uplands of Wales. Some of these are related, but can be distinguished because each has been selected for particular characteristics in closed populations. The Hill Radnor is one of the larger breeds in this group. It retains the vigorous, active nature of upland sheep, together with a relatively coarse and kempy fleece, which gives protection against wet and stormy conditions. The face and legs are a tan or greyish-red colour; the ewes are hornless but the rams are usually horned. However, the horns can often be fairly small, as on the ram lamb shown here.

## Balwen

The severe winter of 1947 caused serious losses among many hill and mountain breeds of sheep. The Balwen was already endangered, and following that year, its numbers fell extremely low. Since then, it has recovered very slowly, and has started to spread in small numbers to other parts of Wales and even into England. All present-day Balwen sheep trace their ancestry to a flock that survived in the original area of the breed in the Tywi Valley in south Wales. It has been claimed that they were introduced by Irish sea pirates, who settled in the upper Tywi Valley. This three-year-old ewe from Dyfed was Breed Champion at the Rare Breeds Show & Sale in 1993, and shows the typical colour pattern of the breed – black or dark fleece and body with a white blaze, white socks and a part-white tail.

Sheep and Goats

**Brillenschaf**

The Corinthian sheep is a native of Austria, and belongs to the Lop-Eared Alpine group of breeds. In Germany, it is found mainly in the south-east of Bavaria and is known as the Brillenschaf, or Kartner Brillenschaf, which means 'spectacled sheep' – referring to the black pigmentation seen around the eyes and on the tips of each ear. It is a mountain sheep, and is adapted to the high rainfall climate of its native area.

*right*
**Jacob**

The alternative name for the Jacob sheep (used in the late nineteenth and early twentieth centuries), is the Spanish, and this provides a clue to its Iberian ancestry. Thus it is likely that it is related not so closely to the British multi-horned breeds, such as the Manx Loghtan and Hebridean, as it is to the multi-horned breeds of the Americas, such as the Navajo-Churro, which were also derived from Iberian foundation stock. The breed has also claimed a Biblical origin, on the basis of Jacob's selection of spotted sheep in the flocks of Laban. The spotted fleece is a hallmark of the breed, and the black wool grows rather longer than the white. The distinctiveness of the face pattern of black cheeks and a white blaze is further augmented by the impressive horns, powerfully swept upwards above the head and curled at the side.

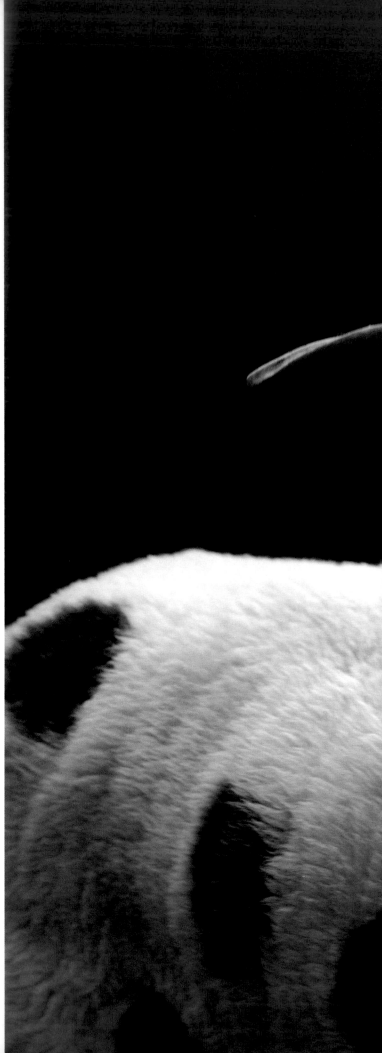

## Southdown

The original heathland sheep of south-east England was a small, active animal. A breeding programme to improve them was put into practice in the late eighteenth century by John Ellman of Glynde in Sussex and later by Jonas Webb of Babraham, near Cambridge. The work of these two men created the Southdown breed of sheep as a small, thickset, compact sheep with tight, close wool. It was destined to exert a powerful influence on sheep breeding in many parts of the world, and the Southdown sheep now found in New Zealand and France are very typical of the early breed. Ridings Twinflower III is from East Sussex, the native area of the breed.

*previous page left*

## Hebridean

When the Hebridean breed first became known outside its island home, it was prized mainly for its aesthetic value, and flocks of these dramatic black sheep graced the parkland areas surrounding many stately homes in Scotland and England. Its appeal was accentuated by its pale amber eyes, which contrasted with its dark fleece and gave it a rather sinister appearance, and by the abundance of horns carried by some animals. The Hebridean is one of the breeds that can have two or occasionally even three pairs of horns. Elliott, the ram from the flock at Wimpole Home Farm near Cambridge, is two-horned, but he has all the other characteristics of the breed, including lustrous black wool. Recently, the Hebridean has demonstrated a special ability to graze and browse tough herbage, and has proved of considerable value in ecological projects where it is necessary to control invasive scrub and weeds.

*previous page right*

## Portland

In earlier times, the chalk downs of Dorset were heavily populated by a small breed of sheep which was a recent descendant of the original tan-faced sheep that inhabited much of Britain. Unfortunately, the glamorous myth that the ancestors of the breed swam ashore from the wrecks of the Spanish Armada cannot be substantiated. However, it is true that whenever King George III visited Dorset, he invariably chose to dine off Portland mutton, and in the mid-nineteenth century D. Low, the agricultural commentator, reported that 'their mutton is exceedingly delicate'.

The face and legs of the Portland are tan, but the shade may vary. The horns of the rams are strongly spiralled, and often have a narrow black stripe running down their length. Otherwise, there should be no black marks, either in the fleece or on the body, as all the pigmentation is red.

Sheep and Goats

### Shropshire

Early in the twentieth century the Shropshire was a very popular breed and enjoyed the benefits of a thriving export market, especially to North America. The sudden decline of this market led to the current endangered status of the breed, from which it is now slowly recovering. It originated in the Welsh Borders as a result of crossing improved breeds, such as the Leicester and Southdown, with local Long Mynd and Morfe Common sheep. This pair are from flocks in Worcestershire. The shearling (a young animal that has been shorn only once) ewe on the left, Frenchlands Isabella, was the Champion Ewe at the Rare Breeds Show & Sale in 1993, and the two-shear ram, Shieldaig Symphony, was Champion Ram at the same event.

## Wiltshire Horn

The Wiltshire Horn is a breed in exile. It became extinct in its native county *circa* 1820, and was relocated in Northamptonshire in the English Midlands, and the Isle of Anglesey off the north coast of Wales. It is a most unusual sheep as it does not grow a fleece of wool. Instead, it develops a matted covering of hair, which peels off naturally. Both sexes have horns, and those of the rams are particularly impressive, but Athelson 20, who was the best ram lamb at the Rare Breeds Show & Sale in 1993, has not yet developed the fully spiralled horns he will carry as an adult.

*left*

**Greyface Dartmoor**

Most longwool breeds in Britain were influenced to some degree by the Dishley Leicester, but the Greyface Dartmoor has retained some distinctive characteristics. This two-shear twin ram from the Bullhornstone flock in Devon has the coarse, wavy wool and powerful head and neck typical of the breed. His owner, Mr J. W. Mead, carries a typical shepherd's crook.

*above*

**Wensleydale**

Herds and flocks of livestock played an important part in the life of the Cistercian abbeys of the Yorkshire Dales in earlier times, and longwool sheep probably had a major role in their systems of management. It is probable that milk from the monks' sheep flocks was used to produce Wensleydale cheese. However, the Wensleydale breed, as it exists today, was not established as a recognizable breed until the early nineteenth century. In 1839, the mating of a Dishley Leicester ram and a Teeswater ewe produced a ram with a distinctively blue-pigmented face. This animal, which was known as Blue Cap, exerted a powerful influence on the development of the Wensleydale, and his colour became a hallmark of the breed. The wool of the Wensleydale is longer and more lustrous than that of any other breed. The fine staples of wool fall in long ringlets, and its high lustre makes it valuable for such diverse uses as tapestry weaving or the manufacture of coat linings.

Sheep and Goats

*right*

**Leicester Longwool**

During the second half of the eighteenth century,
Robert Bakewell (see page 43) started a series of
breeding programmes with several species of farm
animals in order to produce types more suited to the
nutritional demands created in Great Britain by the
Industrial Revolution. His work with sheep led to
the creation of a new breed, known as the Dishley
Leicester, which not only influenced the
development of sheep breeds in Britain and other
parts of the world, but was also the direct ancestor of
the modern Leicester Longwool breed. This
Leicester Longwool, from the Cotswold Farm Park
in Gloucestershire, shows typical pigmentation of
the mainly white face and ears.

*overleaf*

**Lincoln Longwool**

It is possible that polled, white-faced, longwool
sheep were brought to Britain by the Romans. The
ancient breed of Lincoln Longwool may have
originated in an area of Roman settlement. It is a
large animal, and is noted for the heaviness of its
fleece. One ram is recorded as having produced a
fleece weighing 21kgs and a yearling ewe produced a
fleece with a 'staple' length (the length of the fibres
in a lock of wool) of 81cms. The Lincoln has been
exported to many other countries, especially in
eastern Europe, South America and Australasia,
where it was crossed with the Merino and became an
ancestor to several very important Australasian
breeds, such as the Corriedale and the Polworth.

*above*

**Cotswold**

The Cotswold has been strongly influenced by the Leicester Longwool in its development, and now closely resembles its parent breed. It takes its name from its native region which, being literally translated, means 'sheepfold' and 'bare hill'. The Cotswold became severely endangered during the middle of this century, and by 1950 only one flock remained, owned by William Garne of Aldsworth in Gloucestershire. Oakhill Panther, a tall shearling born as a twin, was the best ram at the Rare Breeds Show & Sale in 1993. He is seen here with a short fleece and forelock after shearing.

## Castlemilk Moorit

In the early years of the twentieth century, the Buchanan-Jardine family carried out active breeding programmes on their Castlemilk estate in south-west Scotland, and were specifically interested in animals that were brown in colour. The breed of sheep they developed has now been given the name of Castlemilk Moorit, to denote its place of origin and its colour ('moorit' is derived from a Norse word meaning 'peat-brown' or 'moor-red'). It is a typical primitive sheep breed of northern Europe, horned in both sexes, short-tailed, alert and active. Its colour pattern is the same as that of wild Moufflon sheep, being brown with paler marks on the face and legs and paler wool on the underside and rump patch. The shearling ram Icomb Bobby was born as a twin, and was the best ram of his breed at the Rare Breeds Show & Sale in 1993.

### North Ronaldsay

About 150 years ago, a tall wall was built on the
island of North Ronaldsay, the northernmost island
of the Orkney archipelago, to separate the shore from
the cultivated fields. The native sheep were thus
excluded from the fields by the wall, and in the
intervening period have become totally adapted to an
exclusive diet of seaweed. This has caused significant
physiological changes in the sheep. Otherwise, the
North Ronaldsay is a typical primitive breed of the
north-western fringes of Europe. The wool may be a

variety of colours, ranging through white, grey and
black to brown, and the rams carry impressive spiral
horns which are distinctively ridged and often grow
in alternate bands of pale and dark colour.

Because the total population of this breed was
located on one island, it was very vulnerable, both to
disease and to oil slick pollution from the oilfields in
the North Sea. The Rare Breeds Survival Trust has
purchased another island, Linga Holm, and a group
of breeding sheep to create a reserve population.

Sheep and Goats

89

*above*

**Graue Gehornte Heidschnucke**

The Heidschnucke is a primitive breed of German sheep, probably descended from the same type as the Hebridean in Great Britain. It is associated particularly with Luneberg Heath in north-west Germany (the literal translation of its name is 'heather sheep') and, like the Hebridean, it has considerable value in ecological projects. Some types are white in colour and some are hornless, but

these animals are typical of the Graue Gehornte Heidschnucke, having a grey body with a dark neck and belly and a black face and legs. It is horned and has a short tail. Breeds that have retained distinctive behavioural and grazing characteristics are an important genetic resource, and are likely to assume increasing importance in the future. It has the alert, independent nature of active heathland sheep.

*above*

### Soay

Of all the primitive breeds of sheep, perhaps the Soay bears the closest resemblance to its wild ancestor, the Moufflon. It is a small brown sheep which retains many behavioural characteristics more typical of wild than of domesticated sheep. All Soay sheep are descended from a feral flock which existed on the island of Soay (literally 'sheep island') in the St Kilda group, beyond the Outer Hebrides in the Atlantic Ocean. A few animals were transferred from Soay to the mainland in earlier times, but the main transfer was of 107 animals (20 rams, 44 ewes, 22 ram lambs and 21 ewe lambs) to the island of Hirta, the largest in the St Kilda group, when its human population was evacuated in 1932.

Simon, the stock Soay ram at Wimpole Home Farm, has the powerful horns, dark colour with a moufflon pattern, short tail and hairy mane over his withers that are so typical of the breed. The spirit of independence and aggression in this primitive breed is particularly evident at mating time, and at any time of year it is very difficult to herd them with sheepdogs as, unlike other sheep, they tend to scatter rather than group together when threatened.

*above*

**Schwarzhal**

The Schwarzhal goat derives its name from its highly distinctive and attractive colour pattern. Its hindquarters are white and its forequarters black, with the dividing line at its mid-section. A herd of these uniformly marked animals make a dramatic impact in their Alpine habitat. The breed originated in the canton of Valais in Switzerland (it is also known as the Valaisanne à Col Noir, or the Walliser), but it has spread into the Rhône valley in France. It was seriously endangered at one stage, but is now making a strong comeback as a hardy, thrifty mountain goat; although its milk production is not as high as that of some of the more specialist dairy breeds of goat.

## Pyrenean Mountain

A mountain habitat has proved a mixed blessing for
many breeds. On the one hand, their isolation and
the relatively poor productivity necessitated by their
habitat has prevented them from achieving wider
recognition and popularity. On the other, they have
been protected to some degree from the rapid
changes in the livestock industry that have led to the
extinction of many breeds. Pyrenean Mountain goats
have survived, but only in small numbers, found in
the Spanish and French Pyrenees and in the
Cantabrian mountains in Spain. Like most breeds of
goat, they are naturally browsing animals, and in
some areas, where the density of animals is too great,
this has led to the elimination of trees and bushes and
in extreme cases to desertification. The Pyrenean is a
true mountain breed; usually it has long hair and is
used for both dairy and meat production. Its colour
should be dark brown or black, with paler lower legs
and belly. It is sometimes also known as the Bearnis.

*previous page*

## Bagot

The Bagot goat has been associated for several
centuries with Blithfield Hall in Staffordshire, which
is owned by the Bagot family. It is reputed that the
ancestral stock of the breed was brought back by the
Crusaders as they passed through Europe on their
return from the Holy Land. There is a similarly
marked breed, the Schwarzhal (see page 92), in
Switzerland. However, there are also goats with this
colour pattern among feral herds in Britain, which
provides another possible origin for the Bagot.

A group of Bagots was released as an experiment
on the Rhinog Mountains in North Wales, and have
established a distinctive herd of feral goats in that
area. The foundation herd at Blithfield Hall was
donated to the Rare Breeds Survival Trust in 1979,
and the Trust is now responsible for the conservation
of the breed. The Bagots' long hair is mainly white
on the hindquarters and black on the head and
shoulders, although most animals have a white blaze.
The horns of the males are imposing and are usually
slightly splayed at their tips.

### Girgentana

Although the Girgentana goat is a native of Sicily, its unusual appearance has ensured its place in locations far distant from its original homeland, especially in farm parks. This female is part of a herd at the Tierpark Warder in northern Germany.

Her feminine character is accentuated by the concave profile of her face and her long hair. She also has a pair of toggles, or wattles, on her throat. Her light colour, with some brown markings, is typical of her breed.

**Girgentana**

The vertical spiralled horns of this male are a distinctive characteristic of the Girgentana breed, but his colour is darker than might be expected. The Girgentana is used for dairy purposes, but its yield of milk is not as high as that of specialist dairy breeds. This is due to the fact that it is kept under less favourable conditions in its native area, where it is also known as the Agrigentana.

*above*

**Golden Guernsey**

During the Second World War, the native goats of Guernsey almost became extinct. They were only saved by the determination of a Miss Milbourne, owner of the l'Ancresse herd on the island. Golden Guernseys are a dairy breed, and where they are kept in groups indoors, it is safer for them not to have horns, as they can inflict severe damage on each other. Mott's Jack has no horns, but he has a prominent beard typical of the male. He also has ears which are typically upturned at their tips, and it is possible that the Golden Guernsey may owe part of its ancestry to Mediterranean goats. The Greek historian Herodotus described Syrian goats as having 'wondrous ears [which] turn upwards and outwards at the tips in tribute to Apollo who gave them their golden coats'.

*right*

**Golden Guernsey**

The horns on a mature Golden Guernsey male can be most impressive and play an important role in establishing the dominance between animals, especially at the breeding season. This male has the beard and 'dished' face typical of his breed, but his colour is much paler than that of most Golden Guernsey goats.

# Horses and Ponies

Horses are unusual in that unlike most other species of farm animal,
they were first domesticated by nomadic tribes,
rather than in areas of settled agriculture. It was their use of the horse
that gave these mounted nomads the ability to roam far afield
and make significant conquests of land.
The horse has continued to be associated with war throughout its history, both
as a charger for armoured knights and as a
draught-animal for heavy artillery. It was not until relatively recent times
that it superseded the ox as a source of pulling power in agriculture.
This function itself is now largely redundant, and several old,
traditional breeds of horse are being lost in the quest to develop new
performance sport horses.

## Dales

The Dales pony is one of the largest breeds of moorland and mountain pony in the British Isles. Its size results from some crossing of heavy draught horses, probably Clydesdales, with the native ponies of the Pennines. This influence is betrayed by the hair or 'feather' on the heels, and the Dales pony also possesses an abundant mane and tail. During the first half of the twentieth century, the Dales pony was used as a small draught-horse on many Pennine hill farms, and during the severe winter of 1947 they were the only means of transporting feed to sheep stranded on the isolated moors. In earlier times, the Dales pony was used mainly as a packhorse, carrying 200kg loads of lead from mines in the northern Dales to the coast, in weekly journeys of up to 400kms.

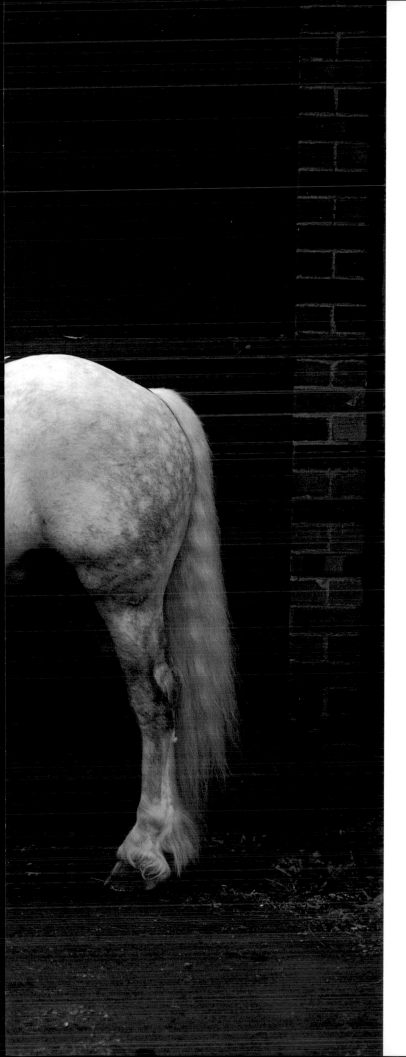

## Dales

Black is the most common colour of the Dales pony, often with one or more white feet, but bay, brown and occasionally grey animals, such as Dark Dale Clint, are seen. These grey animals are probably a legacy of the breeding herds maintained by the Cistercian abbeys in the Yorkshire Dales.

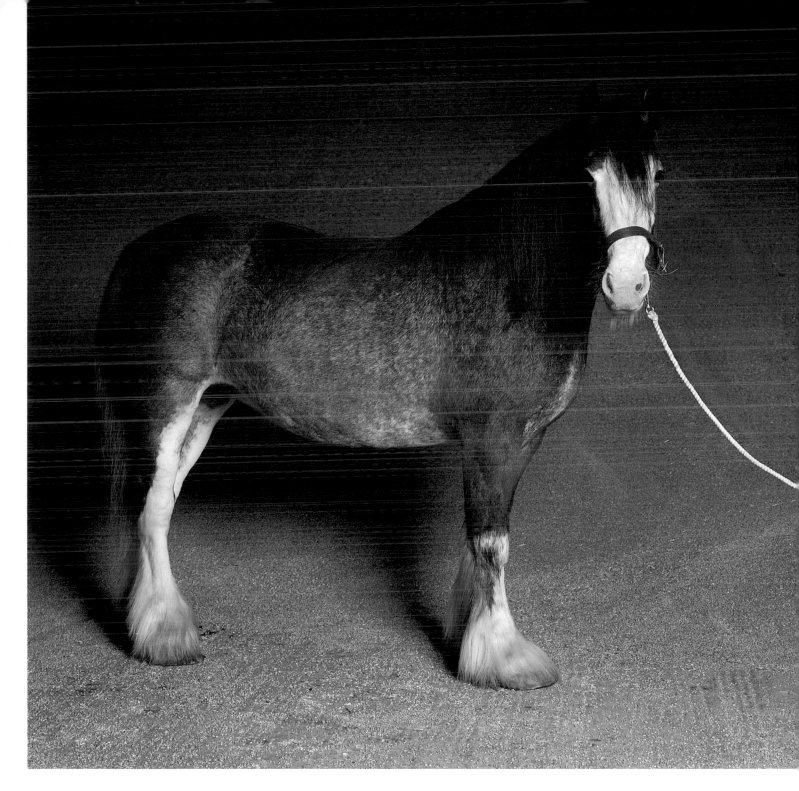

*left*
**Clydesdale**
Scotland did not possess a breed of heavy horse until the middle of the eighteenth century. At that time, imported Flemish stallions were crossed with the large native ponies, and the modern Clydesdale breed developed, to meet the demand created by local industries for greater load-carrying haulage-rather than pack-animals.

*above*
**Clydesdale**
The white blaze, white stockings and roan colour of this mare are common. The abundant hair or 'feather' on the heels is also a typical feature of the Clydesdale, as of the closely related Shire horse, and there has been some intermixing of the two breeds.

*above*

**Schleswig Kaltblut**

Most of the heavy horse breeds of northern Europe are descended from the Ardennes breed of northern France and the Low Countries. Many have been strongly influenced during their development by the large horses of Belgium. The Schleswig Kaltblut is descended from horses which in the Middle Ages carried heavily armoured knights, and this strength proved useful for its later role as an artillery horse and a working draught-animal in agriculture. Although it is a large horse, it is not as massive as its Belgian ancestor, the Brabancon – the *Guiness Book of Records* records that 'Brooklyn Supreme', a Belgian stallion who died in 1948, weighed 1,455kgs and stood 19.2 hands high. The chestnut colour with flaxen mane and blaze of this animal is particularly attractive.

*right*
**Suffolk**

The Suffolk is quite distinct from other British breeds of heavy draught horse, and resembles more closely in type some continental breeds, such as the Percheron. It is clean-legged, and the absence of 'feather' on its heels makes it more suitable for work on the land, as opposed to the Shire, which finds its metier more on hard surfaces as a draught-horse – for example, pulling brewers' drays. The Suffolk is always chestnut or sorrel in colour, and its strong body, carried on relatively short legs, has given rise to its alternative name of Suffolk Punch. It is a powerful, courageous animal, and its pulling power is widely respected. All modern Suffolk horses trace their ancestry to an animal known as Crisp's Horse, which was born in 1768. The breed is promoted through classes at agricultural shows, and the presentation of animals for show requires great expertise and patience, as the braided and decorated mane of Withersfield Charlie (seen here with his owner, Mr Oakley) shows.

*previous page*
**Schleswig Kaltblut**

The Schleswig occurs in various colours and this animal, at the Tierpark Warder in its native province of Schleswig, is bay. It shows liberal growth of hair on its heels, more akin to that of the Shire and Clydesdale of the United Kingdom.

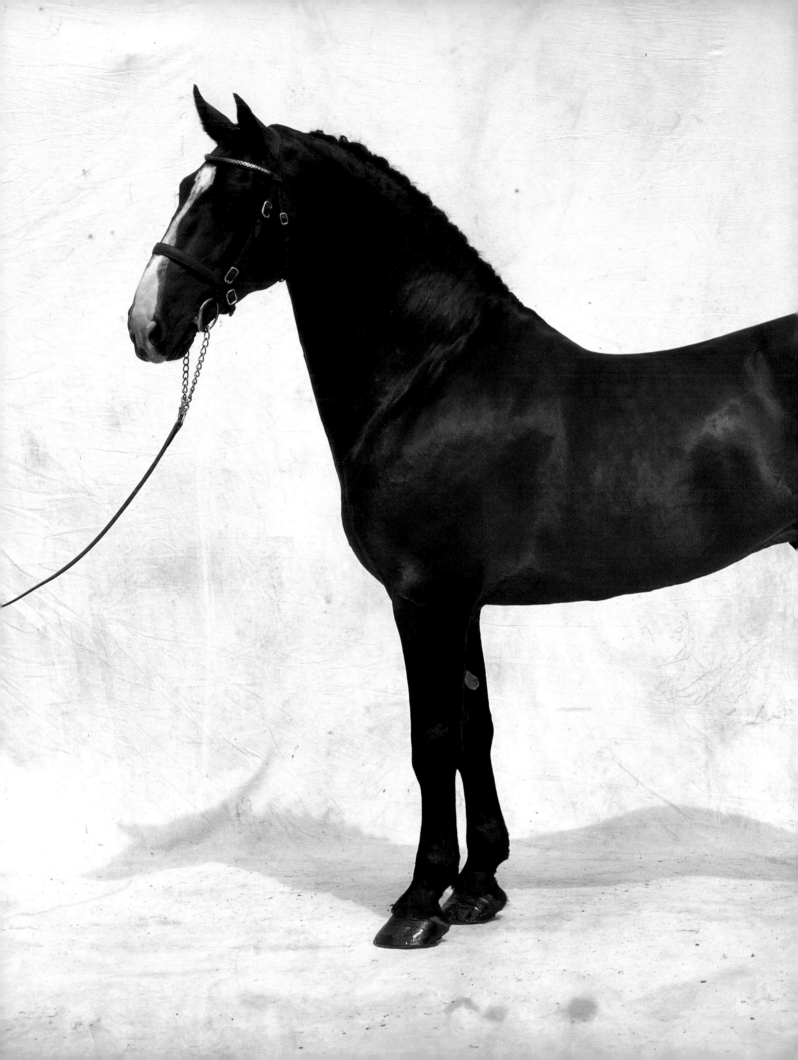

*left*

**Irish Draught**

Banks Fee Daniel, a six-year-old Irish Draught stallion, is considered a fine example of his breed. He has won performance and endurance trials in competition with other breeds and is a prolific sire, having won the breed's Fertility Award. There is some variation within the Irish Draught breed, and it has been changed in type to some degree by introgression from the Thoroughbred. The Irish Draught provides the valuable characteristics of substance, courage and common sense in crossbreeding programmes, and produces high-quality show-jumpers.

*overleaf left*

**Irish Draught**

Daniel himself contains one-eighth (12.5%) Thoroughbred blood, as is evident from his conformation, which is lighter and more elegant than would be expected in a heavy draught breed.

*overleaf right*

**Cleveland Bay**

In earlier times, salesmen in the north of England travelled on horseback, and the most popular riding animal became known as the Chapman horse. This was the foundation of the Cleveland Bay, which evolved as the result of a limited amount of crossing with the Thoroughbred. The Cleveland Bay has become a famous breed, and has been exported to many parts of the world.

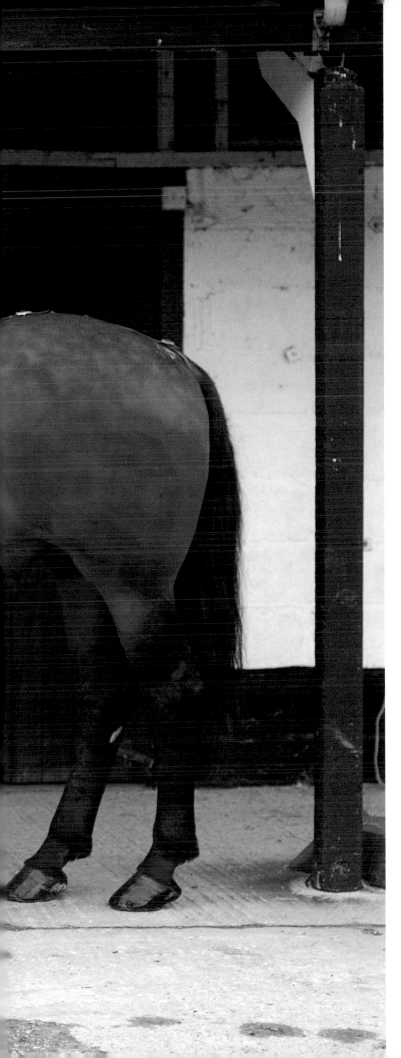

## Cleveland Bay

A number of different types of the Cleveland Bay have evolved. The old-fashioned, short-legged working type is more typical of the original animal, while the more modern, elegant and taller animals, such as Bantry Bere, find a use for hunting, showjumping and carriage-driving, where their strength, temperament and action are of great value. They are always bay in colour.

## Camargue

The Rhône delta in southern France is inhabited by herds of black cattle and grey horses. Both are adapted to their unusual swampy habitat and live in free-ranging breeding groups. The adult Camargue horse is always grey, although the foals may be born a different colour which can persist through the early years. Camargue horses have large hoofs which enable them to travel more easily over their swampy grazing land. They are not easy to domesticate initially, but can prove to be excellent mounts for the cowboys who herd the marshland cattle, being agile and courageous and able to both jump and swim.

*above*

**Eriskay**

Grey is the universal colour of the Eriskay pony, and a grey animal must always have at least one grey parent. However, grey animals also possess the genes for other colours, such as black, bay or roan, and these are seen in the newborn foal. They fade gradually and change to grey in the adult animal. The two older ponies here are watched by a foal of a darker colour, which has not yet faded to the adult shade of grey.

*above*
**Eriskay**

The Highland ponies of Scotland are divided into two distinct types. The Garron is a larger, heavier animal, found on the mainland, while the Western Isles type is smaller and finer. In the late 1960s a few Western Isles ponies were discovered on the island of Eriskay in the Hebrides, and proved to be the last remnants of their type. They were conserved in a carefully monitored breeding programme, and have now been re-established as the Eriskay pony. Like many of the breeds kept in crofting systems in Scotland, the Eriskay is a very tractable and amenable animal.

*overleaf*
**Exmoor**

The migration of horses and ponies from North America through Siberia and Asia to Europe can be traced only in a vague and haphazard manner, but it is very likely that the Exmoor pony represents an ancient type. Bones corresponding very closely to those of the modern breed have been found in the Mendip Hills, close to the Exmoor's present home, from geological levels dating back 60,000 years, and in Alaska from levels dating 100,000 years. The nucleus of the breed now exists in three or four free-ranging semi-feral herds on the unenclosed common land of Exmoor. Their thick coat and abundant mane and tail keep them warm and shed the heavy rain, while their deep jaw and strong teeth enable them to cope with the tough, low-quality grazing. They have a very distinctive face pattern, with a mealy coloured muzzle and cingle (an area of paler colour) around the heavy 'toad' eye. Although Exmoor ponies do not exceed 12.2 hands in height, they are capable of carrying a fully grown man.

Horses and Ponies

*above*
**Baudet du Poitou**
The Baudet du Poitou, or Poitou ass, is notable for
its large size, matched in Europe only by the
Andalucian ass. The Poitou, also known as the
Poitevin, is a most distinctive breed, but during the
1980s almost became extinct. An urgent
conservation programme has been put into action to
save it. It is found in an area facing the Bay of Biscay,
which includes the present departments of
La Vendee, La Vienne and Deux-Sèvres around
Poitiers. An important function of breeds of ass is to
cross with horse breeds in order to produce hybrid
mules. The Baudet du Poitou was used for crossing
with the local breed of horse, the Poitevine
Mulassiere (mule producer) for this purpose.

*right*
**Baudet du Poitou**
The long black or dark brown coat, and the large
floppy ears, also fringed with long hair, give the
Poitou ass a most appealing appearance. Its dark
colour is highlighted by the pale areas around the
eyes and on the muzzle. It has character as well as
looks, and enjoys close communication with its
handler.

# Poultry

Poultry have probably been subjected to the most intensive
breeding selection of any species of farm livestock.
Their breeding is controlled by a small number of international companies,
with birds being bred and selected for intensive methods
of high production, either in battery cages or broiler houses.
The resurgence in the late twentieth century of a consumer demand
for quality products, compatible with high welfare standards
and consideration for the environment, has focused attention once again
on the qualities of the old traditional breeds, which are better adapted
to extensive, rather than intensive, systems of management.

### Light Sussex

When the first poultry show was held at
the Zoological Gardens in London in
1845, it included classes for Old Sussex
fowl, which even at that time had already
been known for several generations. The
Sussex breed was developed most actively
in the second half of the nineteenth
century, particularly in the Heathfield
area of Sussex, for the table poultry
market. There are several colour varieties,
but only three were recognized when the
Sussex Club was formed in 1903, namely
the Speckled, the Light and the Red.
Since that time other colours have been
recognized so that the full range now
includes Brown, Buff, Silver and White.
Although the Speckled was probably the
most typical of the original fowl, the
Light became the most popular, not only
as a productive bird but also because of

its attractive colouration. The base of
white is marked with black on the flight
feathers of the wings, the tail and coverts
(the covering feathers of the tail and
wings), and each feather of the head and
neck hackles is striped with black, as can
be seen on this bantam cock. The White
Sussex was produced as a sport from the
Light variety.

Birds of the true bantam type have no
counterpart among large fowl, and are
restricted to five or six breeds. However,
there are bantam varieties of other
breeds, such as the Sussex, which are
simply miniatures of the large fowl. Their
size is comparable to that of a true
bantam, and a mature Sussex bantam
male would probably weigh less than
1.2kgs, compared with a standard mature
male which would weigh more than 4kgs.

**Silver Dorking**

The Romans discovered native breeds of poultry
when they arrived in Britain. Columella, a Roman
agricultural commentator, writing in 47AD,
described a native breed of fowl that had five toes,
compared to the normal four. These birds were the
forerunners of the modern Dorking breed, which
shares this characteristic and thus has a particularly
ancient lineage. The bird described 2000 years ago
was basically red in colour, but that variety is now
virtually extinct, and most modern Dorkings are
either dark or silver-grey. In other respects it has
remained the same, being a large, robust bird with
a strong body and broad breast, and being noted
for its abundant hackle feathers. The traditional
utility characteristics of the breed are being
conserved by the Rare Breeds Survival Trust in its
Accredited Poultry Scheme, and the Dorking has
shown itself highly suitable for extensive outdoor
systems of management, foraging widely and
having a particular partiality for leatherjackets.

*overleaf left*

**Norfolk Grey**

The Norfolk Grey is a British breed, but of
relatively recent origin. It was previously a popular
breed, particularly in its local area of East Anglia,
but its popularity has now declined. The Norfolk
Grey was also known as the Black Maria, being
silver-white and black with black legs. It is a heavy
bird; a mature cock weighs 3.6kgs. The hens lay
attractive eggs which are brown or with a dark tint.

*overleaf right*

**Derbyshire Redcap**

The indigenous barnyard fowl of northern Britain
was a common sight on many farms until the
middle of the twentieth century. It was a general-
purpose utility bird that foraged on a free-range
system. The Derbyshire Redcap was a typical
example of this type of fowl. It was found mainly in
the southern Pennines, but was very similar to
breeds such as the Yorkshire Pheasant and the
Lancashire Moonie which were found further
north. Historically, it was noted as a very prolific
layer, but in recent times its utility purpose has
declined and it has survived only in small numbers
for exhibition on the showbench. The decline in
the Redcap's utility characteristics has been
accelerated by the great emphasis placed on its
immense and spectacular comb, which attracts 45%
of the total points awarded at shows. The general
colour of the breed is red and black, but each long,
narrow hackle feather of the neck (as here) and
saddle should have a red quill with bottle-green
webbing and black tip and fringe.

### Jubilee Indian Game

The Indian Game was developed as a separate breed in Devon and Cornwall in the early nineteenth century. Its ancestors were the Aseel from India and the Old English Game from Britain. Both these breeds were aggressive and were widely used for cockfighting, but the Indian Game was developed as a less agile, powerful, compact bird, with strong, thick legs. These characteristics were often exaggerated to such a degree that the natural mating of the birds was severely inhibited, and in some strains there was also poor hatchability of the eggs. The Rare Breeds Survival Trust has now established a programme to restore a less extreme type of Indian Game that will be capable of natural behaviour and mating without losing its valuable utility characteristics – for example, the breed is unequalled for the abundance and dense quality of its breast meat. The Jubilee variety was created in 1886, and was named the following year in recognition of Queen Victoria's Jubilee.

**Dark Indian Game**

'Indian Game' is something of a misnomer, as the breed was developed from a mixture of both British and Indian stock. Its alternative name, Cornish Game, is perhaps a more accurate description of its origin. In common with several other large breeds of poultry, a miniature type of Indian Game has been developed, and this bantam cock is an example. Mature bantam males are not expected to exceed 1.3kgs in weight, whereas an adult standard male should weigh over 3.6kgs.

*above*
**Black Croad Langshan**
The Croad Langshan is an imposing dual-purpose breed, used for both eggs and meat, and a mature cock would be expected to weigh more than 4kgs. The legs are feathered down the outer side and, in common with some other Asiatic breeds, its plumage is soft compared to the tight feathering of breeds from northern Europe.

*right*
**Black Croad Langshan**
In 1872, a Major Croad imported some poultry from the Langshan province of northern China. The breed of black fowl that was established from these birds was given the highly appropriate name of Croad Langshan. In 1878 a breeding group passed from the Croad family to the Cloke family, who continued to breed these birds for 115 years until in 1993 Geoffrey Cloke transferred ownership of the group to the Rare Breeds Survival Trust's Accredited Poultry Scheme.

*left*
**Scots Dumpy**
The plumage of the Scots Dumpy may be of several colours but is most commonly either black or 'cuckoo'. By the 1960s, the breed was virtually extinct in Britain, and was only saved by importing birds from a flock in Kenya.

*above*
**Scots Dumpy**
Short-legged fowl have been recorded since 1678, and birds of this type have been known in Scotland for more than two hundred years. They are known alternatively as 'Crawlers' or 'Creepers', and have a distinctive waddling gait. The length of their legs is determined by a genetic factor, and their shanks should not exceed 3.5cms in length. This may make the bird appear deceptively small, but in fact it is medium-sized, and an adult male weighs about 3kgs.

*above*

**Black Croad Langshan**

Each breed of poultry has carefully formulated breed standards which describe a typical bird, and those of the Black Croad Langshan specify black plumage with bluish-black legs but white toenails.

*right*

**White Croad Langshan**

The Croad Langshan was developed by a number of breeders, but particularly by Geoffrey Cloke. An average yield of more than 200 eggs per bird could be achieved under non-intensive farming conditions. The brown eggs also commanded a premium in the market due to their attractive colour. The White Croad Langshan arose as a natural sport in Cloke's flock, and has now been established as a distinct and separate breed. It is the same as its black counterpart in all but the colour of its plumage.

*overleaf*

**Marsh Daisy**

The Marsh Daisy is a British breed, created early in the twentieth century. It resulted from the mixture of four other breeds: the Malay from Asia, the White Leghorn (a member of the Mediterranean group of breeds), the Hamburg (a typical representative of northern European fowl), and the Old English Game from Britain. It was generally considered that the breed became extinct after the Second World War, but it has now been re-established. Originally, it occurred in several different colours and four of these have now been restored – the Buff, Wheaten, Red Wheaten and Black, leaving only White and Brown as colours that may have been lost. The legs have an unusual colour, being pale willow-green.

# Bibliography

Alderson, G.L.H., *The Chance to Survive*, A.H. Jolly Editorial Limited,
Rugby Rare Breeds Survival Trust, Stoneleigh, 1989
—— (ed.), *Genetic Conservation of Domestic Livestock*,
CAB International, Wallingford, 1990
Alderson, G.L.H. and Bodo, I. (eds), *Genetic Conservation of Domestic
Livestock*, CAB International, Wallingford, 1992 (vol. II)
*Animal Genetic Resources Conservation and Management, Animal and
Health Paper 24*, FAO, Rome, 1981
Elwes, H.J., *Primitive Breeds of Sheep and Their Crosses*, Rare Breeds
Survival Trust, Stoneleigh, 1983 (2nd edn)
French, M.H., *et al.*, *European Breeds of Cattle*, FAO, Rome, 2 vols, 1966
Jankovich, M., *They Rode into Europe*, Harrap, London, 1971
Jewell, P.A., *et al.* (eds), *Island Survivors*, Athlone Press, London, 1974
Low, D., *Domesticated Animals of the British Isles*, Longman Green,
London, 1842
Mason, I.L., *A World Dictionary of Livestock Breeds, Types and Varieties*,
CAB International, Wallingford, 1988 (3rd edn)
Porter, V., *Practical Rare Breeds*, Pelham Books, London, 1987
Quittet, E., *Les Races Bovines Françaises*, La Maison Rustique, Paris, 1965
*Rare Breeds Facts and Figures*, Rare Breeds Survival Trust,
Stoneleigh, 1992
Sambraus, H.H., *Atlas der Nutztierrassen*, Eugen Ulmer BGmbH & Co.,
Stuttgart, 1989
Trow-Smith, R., *A History of British Livestock Husbandry*, Routledge and
Kegan Paul, London, 2 vols, 1959
Wallace, R. and Watson, Sir J.A.S., *Farm Livestock of Britain*, Oliver
and Boyd, Edinburgh, 1923 (5th edn)
Wiseman, J., *The History of the Pig*, Duckworth, London, 1986

# Worldwide Rare Breeds Organizations

| | |
|---|---|
| **International** | Rare Breeds International, Avenue Q, National Agricultural Centre, Stoneleigh, Kenilworth, Warks CV8 2LG |
| **Australia** | Australian Rare Breeds Reserve, Snig Hall, Gidgegannup, Western Australia 6555 |
| **Austria** | Verein zur Erhaltung gefahrdeter Haustierrassen, 9010 Klagenfurt, PF.462 |
| **Belgium** | Vereniging Voot het Behoud van Zeldzame Huisdierrassen, Stokstraat 54, B-9688 Maarkedal |
| **Canada** | Joywind Farm Rare Breeds Conservancy, Marmora, Ontario K0K 2MO |
| **Denmark** | Ostergaard, Sct. Ibsvej 3, 4000 Roskilde |
| **Germany** | GEH, Hofbrunnstr 110, 8000 Munchen 71, 2 Vorritzende und Geschaftsstelle |
| | Tierpark Warder, Haustier Schutzpark, Postfach 1205, 2353 Nortorf |
| **Greece** | *IDAAM* Hellenic Institute for Conservation and Utilization of Indigenous Ruminants, Department of Animal Production, Faculty of Agriculture, Aristotle University of Thessaloniki, GR-540 06 Thessaloniki |
| **Netherlands** | Stichting Zeldzame Huisdierrassen, Biologisch-Archeologisch Instituut, Poststraat 6, 9712-ER Groningen |
| **New Zealand** | Rare Breeds Conservancy of New Zealand Inc, PO Box 225, Carterton |
| **Spain** | SERGA, Miguel Servet 177, 50013 Zaragoza |
| **Switzerland** | Pro Specie Rara, Schneebergstrasse 17, CH-9000 St Gallen |
| **United Kindom** | Rare Breeds Survival Trust, National Agricultural Centre, Kenilworth, Warks CV8 2LG |
| **USA** | American Livestock Breeds Conservancy, Box 477, Pittsboro, North Carolina 27312 |
| | Institute for Agricultural Biodiversity, Rural Route 3, Box 309, Decorah, Iowa 52101 |

# Breeders' List

**Frontispiece**
Dark Dorking cock. Wimpole Home Farm,
Old Wimpole, Royston, Herts SG8 OBW

**Page 6**
White Park cow (*Ash Kirsten*). As above.

**Page 11**
Whitefaced Woodland ram (*William*).
As above.

**Page 12**
Exmoor Pony (*Dunsmoor Chaffinch*). Mr and
Mrs N. C. Hill, c/o The Exmoor Pony
Society, Glen Fern, Waddicombe, Dulverton,
Somerset, TA22 9RY
Shetland cow (*Croxteth Alexandra*). Liverpool
City Council, Croxteth Country Park,
Croxteth Hall Lane, Liverpool L12 OH8

**Page 13**
Portland ram (*Percy*). Wimpole Home Farm,
Old Wimpole, Royston, Herts SG8 OBW

**Page 14**
British Lop pig. David Bradley, Home Farm,
Temple Newsam, Leeds, West Yorkshire,
LS15 OAD

**Page 15**
Girgentana goat. Dr J. Gunterschulze,
Deutsche Tierhort Warder, Haustier
Schutzpark, Postfach 1205, 2353 Nortorf,
Germany

**Page 16**
Silver Sussex bantam hen. F. Lund, Handley
Rose Nurseries, Lightwood Road, Marsh
Lane, Sheffield S31 9RE

**Page 17**
White Croad Langshan cock. G. Murch,
Mudds Tenement, Acland Road, Landkey,
Barnstaple, North Devon EX32 OLA

**Page 18**
Tamworth boar (*Thirtleby Green*). David
Bradley, Home Farm, Temple Newsam,
Leeds, West Yorkshire, LS15 OAD

**Page 20**
Tamworth gilt (*Berkswell Lucky Lass 131*).
Boyton Farm Co., Boyton, Warminster,
Wiltshire, BA12 OSS

**Page 20-21**
British Lop pig. David Bradley, Temple
Newsam, Leeds, West Yorkshire
LS15 OAD

**Pages 22-3**
Gloucestershire Old Spots sow and piglets.
As above.

**Page 24**
Gloucestershire Old Spots boar (*Winforton Gerald*). Mr and Mrs M. A. Simpson,
Winforton House, Winforton, Hereford
HR3 6EB

**Pages 24-5**
Gloucestershire Old Spots gilt (*Endsleigh Josephine 810*). Miss C. A. and
Mrs. E. J. Uglow, Edgcumbe, Milton Abbot,
Tavistock, Devon PL19 OQH

**Page 26**
Blonde Mangalitza boar. Dr J. Gunterschulze,
Deutsche Tierhort Warder, Haustier
Schutzpark, Postfach 1205, 2353 Nortorf,
Germany

**Page 27**
Bentheimer sow and piglets.
As above.

**Page 28**
British Saddleback sow. David Bradley,
Home Farm, Temple Newsam, Leeds,
West Yorkshire LS15 OAD

**Page 29**
Berkshire pig. Tilgate Park Nature Centre,
Crawley Borough Council, Tilgate Park,
Crawley, West Sussex RH10 5PQ

**Page 30-31**
Angeln Sattelschwein sow and piglets.
Dr J. Gunterschulze, Deutsche Tierhort
Warder, Haustier Schutzpark, Postfach 1205,
2353 Nortorf, Germany

**Page 31**
Rotbunte pig. As above.

**Page 32**
Large Black pig. David Bradley, Home Farm,
Temple Newsam, Leeds, West Yorkshire
LS15 OAD

**Page 33**
Large Black boar (*Bassingbourn Attempt IV*).
Mrs C. E. Parker, Grange Farm,
Grange Road, Duxford, Cambridgeshire
CB2 4QF

**Page 34-5**
Gascon pig. Philippe Roche, La Combe
Bartas, Sousis, 82150 Montaign de Quercy,
France

**Page 35**
Gascon boar. As above.

**Page 36-7**
Middle White pig. David Bradley, Home
Farm, Temple Newsam, Leeds, West
Yorkshire LS15 OAD

**Page 38**
Middle White gilt (*Smethurst Purity*). R.
Anderton, Smethurst Farm, Smethurst Lane,
Pemberton, Wigan, Lancs WN5 8BL

**Page 39**
Middle White gilt. As above.

**Page 40**
British White cow (*Wimpole Leah*). Wimpole
Home Farm, Old Wimpole, Royston, Herts
SG8 9BW

**Page 42-3**
British White cow. As above.

**Page 43**
Beef Shorthorn (*Bromborough Ben Hur*).
The Bromborough Estate Company Ltd.,
Church Farm, Podington,
nr Wellingborough, Northants NN9 7AS

**Page 44-5**
Red Poll cow (*Capps Chimp*).
Mr and Mrs Oakley, Rede Hall Farm, Rede,
nr Bury St. Edmunds, Suffolk IP29 4UG

**Page 45**
Red Poll bull (*Tatton Red Eric*). Cheshire
County Council, Home Farm, Tatton Park,
Knutsford, Cheshire WA16 6QJ

**Page 46**
Shetland cow (*Croxteth Alexandra*). Liverpool
City Council, Croxteth County Park, Croxteth
Hall Lane, Liverpool L12 OHB

# Index